LONE
PINE

LONE PINE
PUBLISHING

Annuals *for* Michigan

Nancy Szerlag
Alison Beck

The Publisher: Lone Pine Publishing
10145 – 81 Avenue   1901 Raymond Avenue SW, Suite C
Edmonton, AB, Canada T6E 1W9   Renton, WA, USA 98055
Website: www.lonepinepublishing.com

National Library of Canada Cataloguing in Publication Data

Szerlag, Nancy, 1941–
   Annuals for Michigan

   Includes index.
   ISBN 1-55105-346-2

   1. Annuals (Plants)—Michigan. 2. Gardening—Michigan
   I. Beck, Alison, 1971– II. Title.
SB422.S93 2002   635.9'312'09774   C2001-911644-6

Editorial Director: Nancy Foulds
Project Editors: Shelagh Kubish, Dawn Loewen
Editorial: Dawn Loewen, Shelagh Kubish, Dominique Ritter
Illustrations Coordinator: Carol Woo
Photo Editing and Research: Don Williamson, Laura Peters
Production Coordinator: Jennifer Fafard
Book Design: Heather Markham
Layout & Production: Heather Markham, Tina Tomljenovic
Map: Elliot Engley
Cover Design: Rod Michalchuk
Image Editing: Elliot Engley, Jeff Fedorkiw, Tina Tomljenovic, Arlana Anderson-Hale, Ian Dawe
Scanning, Separations & Film: Elite Lithographers Co. Ltd.

Photography: All photos by Tim Matheson or Tamara Eder except AA Selection 87b, 233b, 237a, 239b; Doris Baucom 235b; Joan de Grey 65b, 113b, 177a; Elliot Engley 26b, 29, 30a,b&c, 68c; EuroAmerican 75a, 123b, 125a, 142, 143a, 193a&b, 215a, 234, 235b, 279b; Horticolor ©2001 Nova-Photo-Graphik/Horticolor™ 108, 112; Horticultural Photography/Arthur N. Orans 57b; Colin Laroque 10; Janet Loughrey 223a&b, 231b; Kim Patrick O'Leary 26c, 28, 37c, 47, 56, 78a, 79a, 131a, 143b, 165a&b, 182, 183a&b, 248a, 271a; Peter Thompstone 63a&b, 97c, 134, 135a, 149b, 161b, 179, 180b, 208, 209a&b, 241a&b, 259a&b, 281b.

Front cover photos (clockwise from top left) by Tim Matheson, fuchsia, sunflower, dahlia, gazania, dahlia

Map: frost-date data from National Oceanic and Atmospheric Administration, National Climatic Data Center, Asheville, North Carolina

We acknowledge the financial support of the Government of Canada through the Book Publishing Industry Development Program (BPIDP) for our publishing activities.

PC: P4

Contents

Acknowledgments

WE GRATEFULLY ACKNOWLEDGE ALL WHO WERE INVOLVED IN this project, as well as the many gorgeous public and private gardens that provided the setting for photographs in this book. Special thanks are extended to the following individuals and organizations: Pat Anstett, Allan Armitage, Jeff Ball, Barbara and Douglas Bloom, Thea and Don Bloomquist, Bordine Nursery, Cranbrook Gardens, Cranbrook Garden Auxiliary and the late Hank Szerlag.

Additional thanks to Peter Thompstone for his generous contribution and involvement in preparing this book.

The Flowers at a Glance

PICTORIAL GUIDE IN ALPHABETICAL ORDER, BY COMMON NAME

Abutilon
p. 48

African Daisy
p. 50

Ageratum
p. 52

Agrostemma
p. 56

Alyssum
p. 58

Amaranthus
p. 60

Angel's Trumpet
p. 64

Angel's Wings
p. 68

Baby's Breath
p. 70

Bachelor's Buttons
p. 72

Bacopa
p. 74

Bells-of-Ireland
p. 80

Bidens
p. 82

Begonia
p. 76

Black-eyed Susan Vine
p. 88

Blanket Flower
p. 90

Black-eyed Susan
p. 84

Blue Marguerite
p. 94

Browallia
p. 96

Blue Lace Flower
p. 92

California Poppy
p. 100

Candytuft
p. 102

Calendula
p. 98

Canterbury Bells
p. 104

China Aster
p. 110

Cleome
p. 114

Cathedral Bells
p. 108

Cockscomb
p. 118

Chinese Forget-me-not
p. 112

Coreopsis
p. 126

Cosmos
p. 128

Coleus
p. 122

Cup Flower
p. 134

Dahlberg Daisy
p. 136

Creeping Zinnia
p. 132

Diascia
p. 142

Dusty Miller
p. 144

Dahlia
p. 138

Dwarf Morning Glory
p. 146

Fan Flower
p. 148

Flowering Flax
p. 150

Gazania
p. 158

Geranium
p. 160

Four o'clock Flower
p. 152

Fuchsia
p. 154

Globe Amaranth
p. 164

Godetia
p. 166

Hollyhock
p. 172

Hyacinth Bean
p. 176

Heliotrope
p. 168

Lantana
p. 182

Impatiens
p. 178

Licorice Plant
p. 192

Lisianthus
p. 194

Larkspur
p. 184

Lavatera
p. 188

Livingstone Daisy
p. 196

Lobelia
p. 198

Marigold
p. 202

Million Bells
p. 208

Love-in-a mist
p. 200

Monkey Flower
p. 210

Mexican Sunflower
p. 206

Morning Glory
p. 212

Moss Rose
p. 216

Nasturtium
p. 218

Nicotiana
p. 224

Painted-tongue
p. 228

Nemesia
p. 222

Periwinkle
p. 232

Persian Shield
p. 234

Passion Flower
p. 230

Petunia
p. 236

Phlox
p. 240

Poppy
p. 242

Salvia
p. 246

Statice
p. 256

Stock
p. 258

Scabiosa
p. 250

Snapdragon
p. 252

Strawflower
p. 260

Sunflower
p. 262

Swan River Daisy
p. 266

Sweet Pea
p. 268

Viola
p. 274

Wishbone Flower
p. 278

Zinnia
p. 280

Verbena
p. 270

Introduction

WHETHER YOU PREFER GARDENS WITH GLORIOUS SPLASHES OF color or subtle hints of hues, annual plants are tops in flower power. Easy to grow, these super bloomers are unsurpassed for their versatility and their ability to put on a spectacular, season-long show.

Annuals are plants that complete their entire life cycle in a single growing season. Within one year they germinate, mature, bloom, set seed and die. Many tender perennials, such as geraniums, are unable to survive our cold winters and are also grown as annuals.

Sometimes referred to as bedding plants or transplants, most young annuals are sold in packs of four or six to be planted in bands or drifts in beds, borders and containers. Some newer varieties, such as 'Blue Wonder' Fan Flower, 'Homestead Purple' verbena, 'Surfinia' petunia and the large, colorful Coleus, are sold individually in pots and are called 'premium annuals.' These colorful characters, popular as specimen plants in garden beds as well as in containers, are now an important part of the mix.

Most gardeners in Michigan buy their annuals as transplants, and a sure sign of spring's arrival is the rush of gardeners to local garden centers, greenhouses and farmers' markets to look for new and exciting plants. And how we Michiganders love our annuals: our state ranks third nationwide in the production of annual plants.

Michigan boasts an excellent climate for growing most annuals. These plants usually thrive in our summers, which offer warm temperatures both day and night. Some annuals, however, cannot handle the hottest part of the season and will stop flowering or even die back. The choice then becomes whether to replace them or to cut them back until cooler temperatures prevail, when many will revive and bloom again. Keeping such heat-sensitive plants well watered and planting

most do best when their soil is kept moist and mulched.

The season length in Michigan varies, with the last frost of spring falling any time from late April to late May (see map, p. 13) and the first frost of fall from September to November, depending on where you garden. Most gardeners in Michigan can expect a frost-free period of at least four or five months, which gives annuals plenty of time to mature and fill the garden with abundant color.

Many annuals adapt well to a variety of growing conditions, from hot, dry sun to cool, damp shade. Because annuals are temporary and inexpensive, they are fun for both beginners and experienced gardeners to experiment with. They can be replaced easily if they prove undesirable or extend past their prime.

A decade ago, a pot of petunias, marigolds or geraniums might have sufficed as an annual planting, but today the trend is collections: mixing flowers and foliage to create a tapestry of color and texture. In recent years, thanks to new technology and a burgeoning interest in unusual annuals, hundreds of new varieties have been developed. In addition to brilliant color, these introductions offer improved weather tolerance, new growth habits and extended bloom times. Not only can we select new varieties of old favorites, but we can find new species introduced from all over the world.

In counterpoint to all this novelty, some gardeners are turning to the past to see what was popular in our

them where they will be protected from the hot afternoon sun may help reduce the heat stress and keep them in bloom. Gardeners in the somewhat cooler north and Upper Peninsula often have more success getting heat-sensitive plants, such as Pansy, Lobelia and Candytuft, to stay in bloom over the summer months.

Rainfall is generally quite reliable in Michigan, thanks to the proximity of the Great Lakes, but in recent years many areas have suffered some drought. Annuals generally have shallower roots than perennials and require more frequent watering. Some annuals tolerate drought, but parents' and grandparents' gardens. With the increased interest in organic gardening, and in response to concerns about overhybridization, the use of heritage varieties is on the upswing.

As well, gardeners are no longer simply seeking an instant color fix; they are choosing annuals for their summer-long potential. Some beautiful plants such as Globe Amaranth, overlooked because they bloom later in summer, are now enjoying wider use.

Some new varieties may experience a short period of popularity, but, failing to meet the expectations of the gardening public, fall by the wayside. Others join the ranks of the favorites. Greatly improved varieties—those that have performed exceptionally well in test gardens across the United States and Canada—may be judged by members of the horticultural industry 'All-America Selections Winners.' They usually carry the AASW seal and are worth seeking out.

Average Last-Frost Date

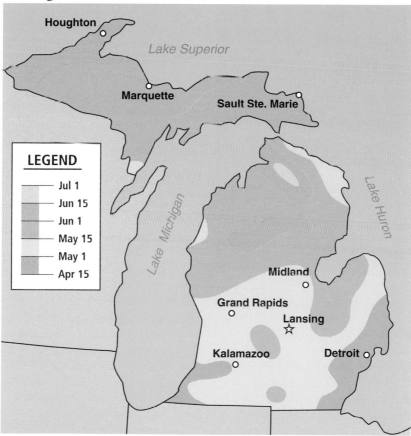

Houghton

Lake Superior

Marquette

Sault Ste. Marie

LEGEND

- Jul 1
- Jun 15
- Jun 1
- May 15
- May 1
- Apr 15

Lake Michigan

Lake Huron

Midland

Grand Rapids

Lansing

Kalamazoo

Detroit

Annual Gardens

borders, as the main attraction in a new garden or in combination with trees, shrubs, perennials and even vegetables. Annuals work magic in gardens that might otherwise suffer from sporadic bloom.

Because different annuals bloom at different times during the growing season, including a variety of these plants in the garden provides continuous color. Annuals are also perfect for filling in bare spaces around small or leggy shrubs or between perennials that come up late in the season. Include annuals anywhere you would like variety and an extra splash of color—in pots staggered up porch steps, in windowsill planters or in hanging baskets. Even well-established gardens are brightened with the addition of annual flowers.

The short lifespan of annuals allows gardeners a large degree of flexibility and freedom when planning a garden. Where trees and shrubs form the permanent structure or 'bones' of the garden, and perennials and groundcovers fill the spaces between them, annuals add bold patterns and bright splashes of color. Annuals give gardeners the opportunity to make the same garden look different each year. Even something as simple as a planting of impatiens under a tree can be made different each year by varying heights and color combinations and by adding different foliage plants for contrast.

ANNUALS ARE TREASURES OF the garden, valued for their ability to provide brilliant color throughout the growing season. Some bloom right through from the first day of planting to a killing frost of fall. Michigan gardeners are constantly finding new ways to include annuals in their gardens, using them as accents in established

When planning your garden, look to a variety of sources for inspiration.

In addition to garden centers, check out books, magazines and plant and seed catalogs. The websites of plant brands, such as Proven Winners at <www.provenwinners.com> or Goldsmith Seeds at <www. goldsmithseeds.com>, showcase the newest varieties and give suggestions for combinations and uses.

As you drive through neighborhoods, study the landscapes. If you see something you like, take notes or a snapshot. If you see the resident gardener, don't hesitate to stop and chat; most people love to show off their gardens and share their expertise.

Annuals enhance all types of gardens. To complement the tidy symmetry of a formal garden, add only a few types of annuals or choose annuals with one flower color. To add a relaxed touch to neat plantings of trees and shrubs, include several different species and colors of annuals. To create an informal, cottage-style garden, you can use a riot of contrasting colors and textures. The same informal garden can be made less chaotic if you allow one or two colors to dominate.

Colors have different effects on our senses. Cool colors, such as purple, blue and green, are soothing and make a small garden appear larger. Annuals with cool colors include Lobelia, Ageratum and Browallia. If you lead a hectic life and need to relax when you are at home, sitting in a garden of cool-colored flowers will help. Warm colors, such as red, orange and yellow, stimulate the senses and appear to fill larger spaces. Warm colors can make even the grandest, most imposing garden

seem warm and welcoming. Annuals with warm colors include Calendula, the salvias and the cockscombs.

If you work long hours and have time to enjoy your garden only in the evenings, consider pale colors such as white, yellow and lime green. These colors show up well at dusk and even at night. Some plants, such as Moonflower (one of the morning glories) and 'Only the Lonely' nicotiana, have fragrant flowers that open only in the evenings.

The key is often to create some contrast between colors in the garden. Chocolate-colored cosmos and burgundy salvias tone down the heat of vibrant red dahlias. Blue Heliotrope or Love-in-a-mist contrasts strongly with orange marigolds or red begonias.

When choosing annuals, most people make the color, size and shape of the flowers their prime considerations. It is also important to consider the size and shape of the

entire plant and its foliage. Colorful foliage is all the rage in Michigan gardens, and the mantra of many new-millennium gardeners is 'leaves, glorious leaves.' Leaves come in all colors, shapes and sizes, and they can set the tone in the garden.

Many annuals boast both beautiful flowers and colorful foliage; snapdragons and begonias, for example, are available with dark red flowers and bronzy purple foliage. Some geraniums, too, have lovely variegated leaves that represent as much a design element as their blossoms.

Annuals with Interesting Foliage

Amaranthus 'Illumination'
Begonia
Coleus
Dusty Miller
Licorice Plant
Nasturtium
Persian Shield
Sweet Potato Vine

Texture is another important element to consider. Both flowers and foliage have a visual texture. Larger leaves can appear coarse in texture, and they can make a garden appear smaller and more shaded. Coarse-textured flowers appear bold and dramatic and can be seen from farther away. Small leaves appear fine in texture, and these create a sense of increased space and light. Fine-textured flowers appear soothing. Sometimes the flowers and foliage of a plant have contrasting textures. Using a variety of textures adds interest and drama to the garden.

Combining a variety of plants whose flowers and leaves encompass different sizes, shapes, colors and textures will make a stunning statement. You will find the Quick Reference Chart on p. 284 useful as you plan for diversity in your garden.

Fine-textured Annuals

Alyssum
Bacopa
Dahlberg Daisy
Lobelia
Swan River Daisy

Coarse-textured Annuals

Dahlia (large-flowered)
Joseph's Coat Amaranthus
Sunflower
Sweet Potato Vine
Zinnia

'Teddy Bear' Sunflower

Getting Started

FINDING JUST THE RIGHT annuals for your garden requires creativity and experimentation. It also requires planning. Before you start shopping or planting, consider the growing conditions in each area of your garden. For your plants to thrive, it's important that their specific needs be coordinated with the microenvironments in your garden. The plants will be healthier and less susceptible to problems if grown in their preferred conditions. It is difficult to significantly modify your garden's existing conditions; match the plants to the garden instead.

The levels of light, the porosity, pH and texture of soil, and the amount of exposure in your garden provide guidelines for selecting your plants. Sketching your garden will help you visualize the various conditions. Note any shaded, low-lying, wet, exposed or windy areas. Understanding your garden's growing conditions will help you learn to recognize which plants will perform best, saving you money and time. Conversely, experimenting with different annuals will help you learn about the conditions of your garden. Consult the Quick Reference Chart on p. 284.

Light

Four levels of light may be present in a garden: full sun, partial shade, light shade and full shade. Available light is affected by buildings, trees, fences and the position of the sun at different times of the day and year.

Plants in **full sun** locations, such as along south-facing walls, receive direct sunlight for at least six to eight hours a day. **Partial shade** or partial sun locations, such as east- or west-facing walls, receive direct sunlight for part of the day and shade for the rest. **Light shade** locations receive shade for most or all of the day, but some light filters through the leaves of surrounding trees or shrubs. The ground underneath a small-leaved tree, such as a birch, is often lightly shaded. **Full shade** locations, which would include the north side of a house, receive no direct sunlight.

Knowing the quality and quantity of light available in your garden will help you choose plants and their location. Sun-loving plants may become tall and straggly and flower poorly in too much shade. Shade-loving plants may get scorched leaves or even wilt and die if they get too much sun. Many plants tolerate a range of light conditions.

Annuals for Sun
Amaranthus
Cleome
Cockscomb
Cosmos
Geranium
Heliotrope
Marigold
Moss Rose
Statice

Annuals for Shade
Browallia
Busy Lizzie Impatiens
Canterbury Bells
Godetia
Nicotiana
Pansy
Tuberous Begonia

Annuals for Any Light
Black-eyed Susan
Black-eyed Susan Vine
Coleus
Cup Flower
Fan Flower
Licorice Plant
Lobelia
Nasturtium
New Guinea Impatiens
Wax Begonia

Tuberous begonia (above),
Black-eyed Susan (below)

Soil

Most soils in Michigan were deposited by receding glaciers and can vary greatly from garden to garden across the state. The fortunate find themselves with soil that is rich and easy to work with; others find they have to contend with soil of poorer quality, consisting mainly of sand, clay or rock. Poor-quality soil of any type can be improved by adding organic matter, such as sphagnum peat moss, shredded leaves, compost or composted manure.

Good soil is an extremely important element of a healthy garden. Plant roots rely on the air, water and nutrients that are held within soil. Plants also depend on soil to hold them upright. The soil, in turn, benefits in at least three ways: plant roots improve soil texture by breaking down large particles; plants prevent soil erosion by reducing the amount of exposed surface and by binding together small particles with their roots; and plants increase soil fertility when they die and break down, adding organic nutrients to soil and feeding beneficial microorganisms.

Soil is made up of particles of different sizes. Sand particles are the largest. Water drains quickly from sandy soil and nutrients tend to get washed away. Sandy soil does not compact very easily because the large particles leave air pockets between them. Clay particles, which are the smallest, can be seen only through a microscope. Clay holds the most nutrients, but it also compacts easily and has little air space.

Statice

Clay is slow to absorb water and equally slow to let it drain. Most soils are composed of a combination of different particle sizes and are called loams.

Most annuals prefer a soil that is easy to work and that contains a moderate amount of organic material. Keep in mind that some annuals, such as cosmos, poppies, nasturtiums and Moss Rose, prefer soil to be on the dry and infertile side. These plants are good candidates for stony banks, neglected areas far from the hose and anywhere amending the soil is out of the question.

It is important to consider the pH level (acidity or alkalinity) of soil, which influences the availability of nutrients. Most plants thrive in soil with a pH between 6.0 and 7.5. Soil pH varies a great deal from garden to garden in Michigan, though most soils tend to be alkaline.

Before amending your soil, have it tested. Your County Cooperative Extension Service will provide a soil profile that indicates the proper amendments needed to improve the soil in your garden. Alkaline soil can be made more acidic by adding sulfur or iron sulfate. Organic mulches made from pine needles, oak leaves or even peat moss will also lower the pH of alkaline soils. Adding compost to garden soil will help buffer the effects of very high or very low pH. Note, though, that altering the pH of your soil takes a long time, often many years, and is not easy. If you are trying to grow only one or two plants that require soil with a pH different than that in your garden, consider growing them in a container or raised bed, where it will be easier to control and amend the pH as needed.

Drainage, the ability of water to move through soil, is affected by soil type and terrain in your garden. Gravelly soil on a hillside will drain very quickly, while low-lying areas may drain very slowly, if at all. Adding organic matter will improve water retention in fast-draining soil. Drainage may be improved in wet areas by installing a drainage system or by building raised beds. Again, it is often best to work with Mother Nature and to choose plants that will thrive in the conditions you already have.

Canterbury Bells (above), Coreopsis (below)

Annuals for Moist Soil
Bacopa
Canterbury Bells
Cleome
Lavatera
Pansy
Wishbone Flower

Annuals for Dry Soil
Baby's Breath
Bachelor's Buttons
Coreopsis
Cosmos
Marigold
Moss Rose

Exposure

Your garden is exposed to wind, heat, cold and rain, and some plants are better adapted than others to withstand the potential damage of these forces. Buildings, walls, fences, hills, hedges, trees and even tall perennials influence and often reduce exposure.

Heat and wind are the most likely elements to damage annuals. The sun can be very intense and temperatures can rise quickly on a sunny afternoon. Plant annuals that tolerate or even thrive in hot weather in the hot spots in your garden. Look for sheltered spots in the garden when planting tall or weak-stemmed annuals.

Moss-lined hanging baskets are susceptible to wind and heat exposure, losing water from the soil surface and the leaves. Water can evaporate from all sides of a moss basket, and in hot or windy locations moisture can be depleted very quickly. Such baskets look wonderful, but watch for wilting, and water the baskets regularly to keep them looking their best.

Overwatering or too much rain can also be damaging. Early in the season, seeds or seedlings can be washed away in heavy rain; mulch around the seeded area will help prevent this problem. Established annuals, or their flowers, can be beaten down by heavy rain. Most annuals will recover, but some, such as petunias, are slow to do so. Place sensitive annuals in protected areas, or choose plants or varieties that are quick to recover from rain damage. Many of the small-flowered petunia varieties now available are quick to recover from heavy rain.

Frost Tolerance

When planting annuals, consider their tolerance to an unexpected frost. The last-frost and first-frost dates vary greatly from region to region in North America. In Michigan, some southern gardens may have a last frost in April, while some gardens in the north may have a last frost in early June. The map on p. 13 gives a general idea of when you can expect your last frost. Keep in mind that these dates can vary significantly from year to year and within the general regions. Your local garden center should be able to provide information on frost expectations in your area.

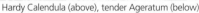
Hardy Calendula (above), tender Ageratum (below)

Annuals are grouped into three categories based on how they tolerate cold weather: hardy, half-hardy or tender. Consult the Quick Reference Chart on p. 284 for hardiness categories of annuals in this book.

Hardy annuals can tolerate low temperatures and even frost. They can be planted in the garden early and may continue to flower long into fall or even winter. I had hardy Calendula planted close to the house and they continued to flower even after a light snowfall covered them. Many hardy annuals are sowed directly in the garden before the last frost date.

Half-hardy annuals can tolerate a light frost but will be killed by a heavy one. These annuals can be planted out around the last-frost date but will generally benefit from being started early from seed indoors.

Tender annuals have no frost tolerance at all and might suffer if the temperatures drop to even a few degrees above freezing. These plants are often started early and not planted in the garden until the last-frost date has passed and the ground has had a chance to warm up. The advantage to these annuals is that they often tolerate hot summer temperatures.

Protecting annuals from frost is relatively simple. Plants can be covered overnight with sheets, towels, burlap or even cardboard boxes. Don't use plastic because it doesn't retain heat and therefore doesn't provide plants with any insulation.

Preparing the Garden

TAKING THE TIME TO PROPERLY prepare your flowerbeds before you plant will save you time and effort over the summer. Many gardening problems can be avoided with good preparation and maintenance. Give your annuals a good start with weeded soil that has had organic material added. For container gardens, use potting soil because regular garden soil loses its structure when used in pots, quickly compacting into a solid mass that drains poorly.

Each spring, loosen your garden soil with a large garden fork and remove the weeds. Avoid working the soil when it is very wet or very dry because you will damage the soil structure by breaking down the pockets that hold air and water. Add organic matter and work it into the soil with a spade or Rototiller.

Organic matter is a small but important component of soil. It increases the water-holding and nutrient-holding capacity of sandy soil and binds together the large particles. In a clay soil, organic matter increases the water-absorbing and drainage potential by opening up spaces between the tiny particles. Common organic additives include compost, grass clippings, shredded leaves, sphagnum peat moss, chopped straw, well-rotted manure and composted bark.

Composting

Any organic matter you add will be of greater benefit to your soil if it has been composted first. Adding composted organic matter to soil adds nutrients as well as improving soil structure.

In natural environments, such as forests or meadows, compost is created when leaves, plant bits and other debris are broken down on the soil surface. This process will also take place in your garden beds if you work fresh organic matter into the soil. However, microorganisms that break down organic matter use the same nutrients as your plants. The tougher the organic matter, the more soil nutrients will be consumed as it is broken down. As a result, your plants will be robbed of vital elements, particularly nitrogen. Also, adding fresh organic matter, such as garden debris, to the garden might introduce or encourage pests and diseases. Composting before adding organic matter avoids these problems.

Compost can be made in a pile, a wooden box or a purchased compost bin. Two methods can be used; neither is complicated, but one requires more effort.

The 'active' or hot composting method requires you to turn the pile every week or so during the growing season. Frequent turning creates compost faster, but because the compost generates a lot of heat, some beneficial microorganisms that help fight diseases are killed. If you prefer the active approach to composting, several good books give step-by-step details of the process.

For most gardeners, the easier method, 'passive' or cold composting, is the more practical approach. Making a passive compost pile involves simply dumping most yard waste into a pile. This organic stuff may include small plants thinned from the vegetable garden, pruned materials cut into small pieces and

leftover grass clippings and fall leaves. Grass clippings should be left on the lawn for the most part, but you can collect them every couple of weeks to add to the pile. Similarly, some fallen leaves should be chewed up with a mulching mower and left on the lawn; some can be collected and used directly as mulch under shrubs and on flowerbeds; and the remainder can be composted. Many gardeners collect leaves from their neighbors, store the leaves in plastic bags and add them to their compost pile over the following year.

Fruit and vegetable scraps from the kitchen may be added to the pile as well, but they attract small animals, which can be a nuisance. Always avoid putting weed seeds and diseased or pest-ridden plants into your compost pile, or you risk spreading problems throughout your entire garden.

After a season or two, the passive pile will have at the bottom a layer of pure black gold, looking much like the leaf mold found in the woods. That is your finished compost. You get to it by moving the top of the pile aside. Spreading the finished compost on the surface of your garden beds will do good things for the soil. Because compost is usually in short supply, many gardeners use it as an amendment just in the planting holes for seedlings, perennials and small shrubs.

Many municipalities now recycle garden wastes into compost that is made available to residents. Contact your local government office to see if this valuable resource is available.

You'll be sure to find worms hard at work in your compost.

Selecting Annuals

MANY GARDENERS CONSIDER the trip to the local garden center to pick out their annuals an important rite of spring. Other gardeners consider starting their own annuals from seed to be one of the most rewarding aspects of gardening. Both methods offer benefits, and many gardeners choose to use a combination of the two. Purchasing plants provides you with plants that are already well grown, which is useful if you don't have the room or the facilities to start seeds. As well, some seeds germinate erratically or require specific conditions that are difficult to achieve in a house. On the other hand, starting from seed may offer you a greater selection of species and varieties, as seed catalogs often list many more plants than are offered at garden centers. Starting annuals from seed is discussed on pp. 29–32.

Purchased annual plants are grown in a variety of containers. Some are sold in individual pots, some in divided cell-packs and others in undivided trays. Each type has advantages and disadvantages.

Annuals in individual pots are usually well established and have plenty of space for root growth. These plants have probably been seeded in flat trays and then transplanted into individual pots once they developed a few leaves. The cost of labor, pots and soil can make them more expensive. If you are planting a large area, you may also find it difficult to transport large numbers of plants.

Painted-tongue

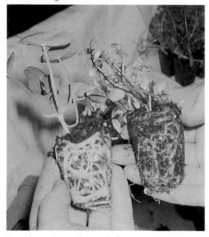

Root-bound seedling on left,
nicely rooted plant on right

Globe Amaranth

Annuals in cell-packs are often inexpensive, and because each pack holds several plants, they are easy to transport. These annuals suffer less root damage when transplanted than do annuals in undivided trays, but because each cell is quite small, plants may become root-bound quickly.

Annuals in undivided trays are also inexpensive. They have plenty of room for root growth and can be left in the trays longer than can plants in other types of containers. Their roots, however, tend to become entangled, making the plants difficult to separate.

Regardless of the type of container, the best plants to choose are often not yet flowering. These plants are younger and are less likely to be root-bound. Check for roots emerging from the holes at the bottom of the cells, or gently remove the plant from the container to look at the roots. In either case, too many roots means that the plant is too mature for the container, especially if the roots are wrapped around the inside of the container in a thick web. Such plants are slow to establish once they are transplanted into the garden.

The plants should be compact and have good color. Healthy leaves look firm and vibrant. Unhealthy leaves may be wilted, chewed or discolored. Tall, leggy plants have likely been deprived of light. Sickly plants may not survive being transplanted and may spread pests or diseases to the rest of your garden.

Once you get your annuals home, water them if they are dry. Annuals growing in small containers may require water more than once a day.

Planting Annuals

ANNUALS ARE AVAILABLE IN stores several weeks before the last-frost date in your area (see map on p. 13), but planting them out in the garden too early can be risky business. Though many seeds can be sowed in the garden at this time, the roots of plants that have been started early indoors can easily be shocked by cold, wet soil. Shocked plants may become stunted and fail to thrive.

The general rule of thumb is to delay planting cold-sensitive annuals, such as begonias and impatiens, until the soil warms to 60° F. An inexpensive soil thermometer can take the mystery out of deciding when it is safe to plant out annuals.

Begin to harden off your newly purchased plants so that they can be transplanted into the garden as soon as possible. Your annuals are probably accustomed to growing in the sheltered environment of a greenhouse, and they will need to become acclimatized to the outdoors. They can be placed outdoors in a lightly shaded spot each day and brought into a sheltered porch, garage or house each night for about a week, or until the last-frost date has passed and the soil has had a chance to warm up.

Once the soil has warmed sufficiently and you have hardened off your annuals, it is time to plant them out. If your beds are already prepared, you are ready to start. The only tool you are likely to need is a trowel. Be sure you have set aside enough time to do the job. You don't want to remove young plants from

their pots and then not finish planting them. If they are left out in the sun, they can quickly dry out and die. It helps to choose an overcast day for planting out.

Moisten the soil to help ease the plants from their containers. The plants may come out by pushing on the bottom of the cell or pot with your thumb. If the plants were growing in an undivided tray, you will

Coreopsis, Dahlia & Marigold

have to gently untangle the roots. Very tangled roots can be separated by immersing them in water and washing some of the soil away. If you must handle the plant, hold it by a leaf to avoid crushing the stems. Remove and discard any damaged leaves or growth.

The rootball should contain a network of white roots. If the rootball is densely matted and twisted, break apart the tangle with your thumbs. New root growth will start from the breaks and spread outwards.

Insert your trowel into the soil and pull it towards you, creating a wedge. Place your annual into the hole and firm the soil around the plant with your hands. Water newly planted annuals gently but thoroughly. They will need regular watering for a couple of weeks until they become established.

You don't have to be conservative when arranging your flowerbeds. Although formal bedding-out patterns are still used in many parks and formal gardens, plantings can be made in casual groups and natural drifts. The quickest way to space out your annuals is to remove them from their containers and randomly place them on the bed. You will then be able to mix colors and plants without too much planning. Plant a small section at a time—don't allow the roots to dry out. This is especially important if you have a large bed to plant.

If you are adding just a few annuals here and there to accent your shrub and perennial plantings, plant in groups. Random clusters of three to five plants adds color and interest.

Combine low-growing or spreading annuals with tall or bushy ones. Keep the tallest plants towards the back of the bed and smallest plants towards the front. By doing so, you will improve the visibility of the plants and hide the often unattractive lower limbs of taller plants. Be sure to leave your plants enough room to spread. They may look lonely and far apart when you first plant them, but annuals quickly grow to fill in the space you leave.

There are no strict rules when it comes to planting and spacing. Whether you like your annuals in straight rows or in a jumble of colors, shapes and sizes, plant according to your preference. Have fun and create something you will enjoy.

Annuals from Seed

STARTING ANNUALS FROM SEED can be fun and can provide you with a wider variety of annuals than that available from garden centers. Dozens of catalogs from different growers offer a diverse selection of annuals that you can start from seed. Many gardeners while away chilly winter evenings by poring over seed catalogs and planning their spring and summer gardens.

Starting your own annuals can save you money, particularly if you have a large area to plant. The basic equipment necessary is not expensive, and most seeds can be started in a sunny window. You may, however, encounter a problem of limited space. One or two trays of annuals don't take up much room, but storing more than that may be unreasonable. For this reason, many gardeners start a few specialty plants themselves but purchase the bulk of their annuals as bedding plants.

Most annuals are started from seed indoors in late winter or early spring, about six to eight weeks before the last-frost date in your area (see map on p. 13). Once the seeds sprout, seedlings left too long indoors without grow lights will become tall, spindly plants that are starved for sunlight and never thrive. Don't start seeds too early; remember, you just want to give them a bit of a head start.

Some annuals have seeds that germinate quickly, and some annual seedlings don't transplant well. Such annuals are best seeded directly in the garden, commonly referred to as

direct sowing or sowing in situ. Most seeds can be sown any time from when the soil is workable to when it has thoroughly warmed. A sowing of cold-tolerant plants in the garden in August will give them time to germinate and color up the garden well into fall.

Each plant in this book will have specific information on starting from seed, but a few basic steps can be followed for all seeds. The easiest way for the home gardener to start seeds is by using cell-packs in trays

Sprouted seedlings with fluorescent light

Watering seeds

Preparing seed trays

with plastic dome covers. The cell-packs keep roots separated, and the tray and dome keep moisture in.

Seeds can also be started in pots, peat pots or peat pellets. The advantage to starting in peat pots or pellets is that you will not disturb the roots when you transplant your annuals. When planting out peat pots, be sure to remove the top couple of inches of pot. If any of the pot sticks up out of the soil, it can wick moisture away from the roots.

If you use a growing mix (soil mix), make sure it is intended for seedlings. These mixes are very fine, usually made from peat moss, vermiculite and perlite. The mix will have good water-holding capacity and will have been sterilized in order to prevent pests and diseases from attacking your tender young seedlings. Fill your pots or seed trays with moist soil mix and firm it down slightly. Soil that is too firmly packed will not drain well. Wet the soil before planting your seeds to prevent them from getting washed around. The easiest method is to wet the soil before you fill the trays or pots.

Large seeds can be planted one or two to a cell, but smaller seeds may have to be placed in a folded piece of paper and sprinkled evenly over the soil surface. Very tiny seeds, like those of begonia, can be mixed with fine sand before being sprinkled across the soil surface. Mixing with sand will more evenly space out the seeds.

Tiny and small seeds will not need to be covered with any more soil, but medium-sized seeds can be lightly covered, and large seeds can be poked into the soil. Some seeds need to be exposed to light in order to germinate; these should be left on or near the soil surface regardless of their size.

Place pots or flats of seeds in plastic bags to retain humidity while the seeds are germinating. Many planting trays come with clear plastic covers that can be placed over the trays. Remove the plastic once the seeds have germinated.

Water seeds and small seedlings with a fine spray from a hand-held mister. Small seeds can easily be washed around if the spray is too strong. I recall working at a green-house where the Alyssum seed trays were once watered a little too vigorously. Alyssum was soon found growing just about everywhere—with other plants, in the gravel on the floor and even in some of the flowerbeds. The lesson is 'water gently.' A less durable species would not have come up at all if its seeds were washed into an adverse location.

Small seedlings will not need to be fertilized until they have about four or five true leaves. Seeds provide all the energy and nutrients that young seedlings require. Too much fertilizer, and/or fertilizer applied too early, causes the plants to develop soft growth that is more susceptible to insects and diseases, and fertilizer that is too strong can burn tender young roots. When the first leaves that sprouted (the seed leaves) begin to shrivel, the plant has used up all its seed energy. You can then begin to use fertilizer diluted to one-quarter strength when feeding

Zinnias can be sowed directly into the garden.

seedlings or young plants. Feed about every two weeks or according to product instructions.

Take care to prevent damping off, a disease caused by soil-borne fungi. An afflicted seedling appears to have been pinched, usually at soil level. The pinched area blackens and the seedling topples over and dies. Using sterile soil mix, keeping soil evenly moist and maintaining good air circulation will usually prevent this problem. It may also help to water small seedlings from the bottoms of their containers with cooled chamomile tea.

If the seedlings get too big for their containers before you are ready to plant them out, you may have to pot them to prevent them from becoming root-bound. Harden plants off by gradually exposing them to the sun, wind and fluctuating temperatures of the outdoors for increasing periods of time every day for at least a week.

Bachelor's Buttons

California Poppy (center), Poppy (below)

To start seeds directly in the garden, begin with a well-prepared bed that has been smoothly raked. The small furrows left by the rake will help hold moisture and prevent the seeds from being washed away. Sprinkle the seeds onto the soil and cover them lightly with peat moss or more soil. Larger seeds can be planted slightly deeper into the soil. You may not want to sow very tiny seeds directly in the garden because they can blow or wash away; large seeds are better choices for direct sowing. The soil should be kept moist, but not soggy, to ensure even germination. Use a gentle spray to avoid washing the seeds around the bed or they will inevitably pool into dense clumps. Covering your newly seeded bed with chicken wire, an old sheet or some thorny branches will discourage animals from digging.

Annuals for Direct Seeding

Amaranthus
Baby's Breath
Bachelor's Buttons
Black-eyed Susan
Calendula
California Poppy
Cleome
Cockscomb
Cosmos
Godetia
Larkspur
Nasturtium
Poppy
Sunflower
Sweet Pea
Zinnia

Caring for Annuals

ONGOING MAINTENANCE WILL
keep your garden looking its best.
Some annuals require more care
than others, but most require minimal care once established. Weeding,
mulching, watering, fertilizing,
pinching and deadheading are the
basic tasks that, when performed
regularly, pay dividends throughout
the season. As well, some plants
grown as annuals are actually perennials and may be overwintered with
little effort.

Weeding

Controlling weed populations
keeps the garden healthy and neat.
Weeding may not be anyone's
favorite task, but it is an essential
one. Weeds compete with your
plants for light, nutrients and space,
and they can harbor pests and diseases.

Weeds can be pulled by hand or
with a hoe. Shortly after a rainfall,
when the soil is soft and damp, is the
easiest time to pull weeds. A hoe
scuffed quickly across the soil surface will uproot small weeds and
sever larger ones from their roots.
Try to pull weeds out while they are
still small. Once they are large
enough to flower, many will quickly
set seed, and you will have an entire
new generation to worry about.

Mulching

A layer of mulch around your
plants will prevent weeds from germinating by preventing sufficient
light from reaching the seeds. Those
that do germinate will be smothered

or will find it difficult to get to the soil surface, exhausting their energy before they get a chance to grow.

Mulch also helps maintain consistent soil temperatures and ensures that moisture is retained more effectively. In areas that receive heavy wind or rainfall, mulch can protect soil and prevent erosion. Mulching is effective in both garden beds and planters.

Organic mulches include materials such as compost, shredded bark, grass clippings or shredded leaves. These mulches add nutrients to soil as they break down, thereby improving the quality of the soil and ultimately the health of your plants.

Spread 2–3" of mulch over the soil after you have planted your annuals. Don't pile the mulch too thickly in the area immediately around the crowns and stems of your annuals. Mulching right up against plants

Mulched garden

traps moisture, prevents air circulation and encourages fungal disease.

As your mulch breaks down over the summer, be sure to replenish it.

Watering

Water thoroughly but infrequently. Annuals given a light sprinkle of water every day will develop roots that stay close to the soil surface, making the plants vulnerable to heat and to dry spells. Annuals given a deep watering once a week will develop a deeper root system. In a dry spell they will be adapted to seeking out the water trapped deeper in the ground.

About 1" of water a week, either from rainfall or a hose, will usually suffice. Be sure the water penetrates several inches into the soil. More water may be needed in very hot weather, when there is no rain. A mulch will prevent water from evaporating out of the soil.

To save time, money and water, you may wish to install an irrigation system. When used properly, irrigation systems save you money by using water more efficiently. They apply the water exactly where it is needed, near the roots, and reduce the amount of water lost to evaporation. Irrigation systems can be very complex or very simple, as simple as laying soaker hoses around your garden beds under the mulch. Consult with your local garden center or landscape professional for ideas.

Annuals in hanging baskets and planters will need to be watered more frequently than plants growing in the ground. The smaller the container, the more often the plants will

Nasturtium & Bacopa

need watering. Containers and hanging moss baskets may need to be watered twice daily during hot, sunny weather.

Fertilizing

Your local garden center should carry a good supply of both organic and chemical fertilizers. Follow the directions carefully because using excessive fertilizer can kill your plants by burning their roots. Whenever possible, use organic fertilizers because they are generally less concentrated and less likely to burn your plants.

Many annuals will flower most profusely if they are fertilized regularly. Some gardeners fertilize hanging baskets and container gardens every time they water, using a very dilute fertilizer so as not to burn the plants. Too much fertilizer can result in plants that produce weak growth that is susceptible to pest and disease problems. Some plants, like nasturtiums, grow better without fertilizer and may produce few or no flowers when fertilized excessively.

Fertilizer comes in many forms. Liquids or water-soluble powders can be used when watering. Slow-release pellets or granules are mixed into the garden or potting soil or sprinkled around the plants and left to work over the summer.

Grooming

Good grooming will keep your annuals looking neat, make them flower more profusely and help prevent pest and disease problems. Grooming may include pinching, staking, trimming and deadheading.

Pinch out (remove by hand or with scissors) any straggly growth

Impatiens are self-cleaning.

or tomato cages. Insert the twigs or cages around the plant when it is small and it will grow to fill in and hide the stakes.

If annuals appear tired and withered by mid-summer, try trimming them back to encourage a second bloom. Mounding or low-growing annuals, like petunias, respond well to trimming. Take your garden shears and trim back one-quarter to one-half of the plant growth. New growth will sprout along with a second flush of flowers.

Deadheading, or removing faded flowers, is important in maintaining the health of annuals and in prolonging their bloom. Get into the habit of picking off spent flowers as you are looking around your garden; a little deadheading each day will save you a big job later. Some plants, such as impatiens and wax begonias, are self-cleaning, meaning that they drop their faded blossoms on their own and don't need deadheading.

and the tips of leggy annuals. Plants in cell-packs may have developed tall and straggly growth in an attempt to get light. Pinch back the long growth when planting out to encourage bushier growth.

Some annuals have very tall growth naturally and cannot be pinched. Instead, remove the main shoot after it blooms to encourage side shoots to develop. Some tall annuals, like Larkspur, require staking with bamboo or other tall, thin stakes. Tie the plant loosely to the stake; strips of nylon hosiery make soft ties that won't cut into the plant. Stake bushy plants with twiggy branches, peony hoops

Growing Perennials as Annuals

Many of the plants grown as annuals are actually perennials, such as geraniums, that originate in warmer climates and are unable to survive colder winters. Other plants grown as annuals are biennials, such as Canterbury Bells, and are started very early in the year to allow them to grow and flower in a single season. These perennials and biennials are listed as such in the text. You can use several techniques to keep these plants for more than one summer.

Some tropical perennials can be simply brought inside and treated as houseplants in the colder months. A reverse hardening-off process is used to acclimatize plants to an indoor environment. Plants such as geraniums, black-eyed Susan vines and Heliotrope, which are grown in full sun all summer, are gradually moved to shady garden spots. Doing so allows them to develop more efficient leaves, capable of surviving in limited light.

Geranium

The underground parts of tuberous perennials can be stored over winter and re-planted in late winter or early spring. Plants such as dahlias, tuberous begonias and Four-o'clock Flower can be dug up in fall, after the above-ground parts die back but before the ground freezes. Shake the loose dirt away from the roots and let them dry out a bit in a cool, dark place. Once they are dry, the rest of the soil should brush away. Dust the tubers with an anti-fungal powder (found at garden centers) before storing them in moist peat moss or coarse sawdust. Keep them in a cool, dark, dry place that doesn't freeze. Pot them if they start to sprout and then keep them in a bright window and in moist soil. They should be potted by late winter or early spring so they will be ready for spring planting.

Four-o'clock Flower (center), Dahlia (below)

Cuttings can be taken from large or fast-growing plants such as Licorice Plant and the black-eyed Susan vines. Grow late-summer cuttings over winter for new spring plants.

If winter storage sounds like too much work, replace your annuals each year and leave the hard work to the growers.

Problems & Pests

NEW ANNUALS ARE PLANTED each spring, and often different species are grown each year. These factors make it difficult for pests, which may have only one or a few preferred host plants, to establish permanent populations. However, because annual species are often grown together in masses, any problems that do set in over the summer are likely to affect all the plants.

For many years pest control involved spraying or dusting in an attempt to eliminate every garden pest. Experts now suggest a more moderate approach that aims to keep problems and the resulting damage at an acceptable level. As long as your annuals are still flowering and don't appear too chewed up or diseased, the damage should be considered negligible. Chemicals, which cause more harm than good, should be used as only a last resort.

They harm beneficial organisms as well as detrimental ones, leaving the garden vulnerable to greater problems. Chemical-free pest control is also safer for the gardener, family members, pets and wildlife.

An organic approach to managing pests has four components. Cultural controls are the most important. Physical controls should be attempted next, followed by biological controls. Chemical controls should be used only when the first three options have proven unsuccessful.

Cultural controls involve the everyday gardening techniques you use to care for your plants. Choosing varieties of annuals that resist pests and diseases, ensuring that each plant receives good air circulation and preventing competition between plants for light, nutrients and space are all examples of cultural controls.

If pests plague a certain type of plant each year, avoid that species in the future. Keeping garden tools clean and tidying up dead plant matter and fallen leaves at the end of the season are also good practices.

Physical controls, typically used to deal with insect problems, include such tactics as picking insects off plants by hand. This solution is very effective and not too time consuming if you are able to catch the problem at an early stage. Large, slow insects are particularly easy to pick off. Other physical controls include barriers that prevent insects from reaching the plant and traps that catch or confuse the insects. For diseases, the only physical control that may be effective is to remove the infected plant part or possibly the entire plant.

Biological controls make use of natural predators. Birds, snakes, frogs, ladybird beetles and spiders are just a few of the natural predators that can help you manage pest problems in your garden by eating many of the insects that attack your plants. Encourage their presence by installing a birdfeeder or birdbath. Many beneficial insects probably already reside in your yard. Avoid using chemical pesticides, and provide food sources such as nectar-bearing plants (many annuals are nectar producers) to welcome predatory insects to your garden.

Chemical controls are, again, a last resort. Remember that using chemicals also kills the beneficial insects in your garden. If you find chemical controls necessary, consider organic options first. Organic pesticides, while still poisonous, gradually break down into harmless components. Organic chemicals can be purchased at garden centers. Be sure to follow the directions carefully to avoid improper application that could harm your garden, your family or you.

Frogs eat many insect pests.

Glossary of Pests & Diseases

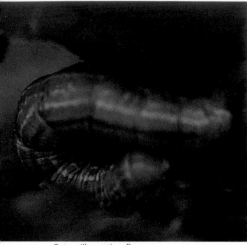

Caterpillar eating flowers

Aphids (center), Ladybird beetle larva (below)

Anthracnose

Fungus. Yellow or brown spots on leaves; sunken lesions and blisters on stems; can kill plant.

What to Do: Choose resistant varieties and cultivars; remove and destroy infected plant parts; thin out stems to improve air circulation; avoid handling wet foliage; keep soil well drained; clean up and destroy material from infected plants at end of growing season.

Aphids

Tiny, pear-shaped insects, winged or wingless; green, black, brown, red or gray. Cluster along stems, on buds and on leaves. Example: woolly adelgids. Suck sap from plants; cause distorted or stunted growth. Sticky honeydew forms on surfaces and encourages sooty mold growth.

What to Do: Squish small colonies by hand; brisk water spray dislodges them; many predatory insects and birds feed on them; spray serious infestations with insecticidal soap or neem oil according to package directions.

Aster Yellows

Disease organisms transmitted by leafhoppers. Cause stunted or deformed growth, yellowed and deformed leaves, dwarfed and greenish flowers; can kill plants.

What to Do: Control insects with insecticidal soap; remove and destroy infected plants; destroy any local weeds sharing the symptoms. Disease cannot be cured.

Beetles

Many types and sizes; usually rounded in shape with hard, shell-like outer wings covering membranous inner wings. Some are beneficial, e.g., ladybird beetles ('ladybugs'); others, e.g., June beetles, leaf skeletonizers and weevils, eat plants. Larvae: see Borers, Grubs. Leave wide range of chewing damage: make small or large holes in or around margins of leaves; consume entire leaves or areas between leaf veins ('skeletonize'); may also chew holes in flowers. Some bark beetle species carry deadly plant diseases.
What to Do: Pick beetles off at night and drop them into an old coffee can half filled with soapy water (soap prevents them from floating and climbing out). Spray heavy infestations with neem oil according to package directions.

Blight

Fungal diseases, many types; e.g., leaf blight, gray mold (Botrytis blight), snow blight. Leaves, stems and flowers blacken, rot and die.
What to Do: Thin stems to improve air circulation; keep mulch away from base of plant; remove debris from garden at end of growing season. Remove and destroy infected plant parts.

Borers

Worm-like larvae of some moths and beetles; vary in size and get bigger as they bore through plants. Burrow into plant stems, leaves or roots; stems weaken and break; leaves wilt; may see tunnels in leaves, stems or roots; rhizomes may be hollowed out entirely or in part.
What to Do: Remove and destroy parts that are being bored; may be able to squish borers within leaves; may need to dig up and destroy infected roots and rhizomes.

Bugs (True Bugs)

Small insects up to $1/2$" long; green, brown, black or brightly colored and patterned. Many beneficial; a few pests, such as lace bugs, pierce plants to suck out sap. Earwigs are usually beneficial but may damage plants if other food is in short supply. Some bugs inject toxins that deform plants; leaves have sunken areas where pierced; leaves rip as they grow; leaves, buds and new growth may be dwarfed and deformed.
What to Do: Remove debris and weeds from around plants in fall to destroy overwintering sites. Spray plants with insecticidal soap.

Caterpillars

Larvae of butterflies, moths, sawflies. Include bagworms, budworms, case bearers, cutworms, leaf rollers, leaf tiers, loopers. Chew foliage and buds. Can completely defoliate a plant if infestation severe.
What to Do: Removal from plant is best control. Use high-pressure water and soap or pick caterpillars off by hand if plant is small enough. Control biologically using the naturally occurring soil bacterium *Bacillus thuringiensis* var. *kurstaki* or *B.t.* for short (commercially available); breaks down gut lining of caterpillars. Can also use neem oil according to package directions.

Cutworms

see Caterpillars

Galls

Unusual swellings of plant tissues. Can affect leaves, buds, stems, flowers, fruit or trunks. May be caused by insects or diseases. Often a specific gall affects a single genus or species.
What to Do: Cut galls out of plant and destroy them. Galls caused by insects usually contain the insect's eggs and juvenile forms. Prevent these galls by controlling insect before it lays eggs; otherwise try to remove and destroy infected tissue before young insects emerge. Generally insect galls are more unsightly than damaging to plants. Galls caused by diseases often require destruction of plant. Avoid placing other plants susceptible to same disease in that location.

Gray Mold

see Blight

Grubs

Larvae of different beetles; commonly found below soil level, curled in C-shape. Body white or gray; head may be white, gray, brown or reddish. Problematic in lawns; may feed on plant roots. Plant wilts despite regular watering; may pull easily out of ground in severe cases.

What to Do: Toss any grubs found while digging onto a stone path, driveway, road or patio for birds to devour; apply parasitic nematodes or milky disease spore to infested soil (ask at your local garden center).

Leafhoppers & Treehoppers

Small, wedge-shaped insects; can be green, brown, gray or multi-colored. Jump around frantically when disturbed. Suck juice from plant leaves. Cause distorted growth. Carry diseases such as aster yellows.
What to Do: Encourage predators by planting nectar-producing species like yarrow. Wash insects off with strong spray of water; spray with insecticidal soap or neem oil according to package directions.

Leaf Miners

Tiny, stubby larvae of some butterflies and moths; may be yellow or green. Tunnel within leaves leaving winding trails; tunneled areas lighter in color than rest of leaf. Unsightly rather than a major health risk to plant.
What to Do: Remove debris from area in fall to destroy overwintering sites; attract parasitic wasps with nectar plants such as yarrow. Remove and destroy infected foliage; can sometimes squish by hand within leaf.

Leaf Spot

Two common types: one caused by bacteria and the other by fungi. *Bacterial:* small speckled spots grow to encompass entire leaves; leaves turn brown or purple and may drop. *Fungal:* black, brown or yellow spots; leaves wither; e.g., scab, tar spot.

Powdery mildew on Zinnia

What to Do: Bacterial infection more severe; must remove entire plant. For fungal infection, remove and destroy infected plant parts. Sterilize removal tools; avoid wetting foliage or touching wet foliage; remove and destroy debris at end of growing season. Spray with neem oil according to package directions.

Mealybugs

Tiny crawling insects related to aphids; appear to be covered with white fuzz or flour. Sucking damage stunts and stresses plant. Mealybugs excrete honeydew that promotes growth of sooty mold.

What to Do: Remove by hand on smaller plants; wash plant off with soap and water; wipe off with alcohol-soaked swabs; remove heavily infested leaves; encourage or introduce natural predators such as mealybug destroyer beetle and parasitic wasps; spray with insecticidal soap. Keep in mind larvae of mealybug destroyer beetles look like very large mealybugs. Spray with neem oil according to package directions.

Mildew

Two types, both caused by fungus, but with slightly different symptoms. *Downy mildew:* yellow spots on upper sides of leaves and downy fuzz on undersides; fuzz may be yellow, white or gray. *Powdery mildew:* white or gray powdery coating on leaf surfaces, does not brush off.

What to Do: Choose resistant cultivars; space plants well; thin stems to encourage air circulation; tidy any debris in fall. Remove and destroy infected leaves or other parts. Use neem oil according to directions.

Snail eating leaf

Mites

Tiny, eight-legged relatives of spiders; do not eat insects, but may spin webs. Almost invisible to naked eye; red, yellow or green; usually found on undersides of plant leaves. Examples: bud mites, spider mites. Suck juice out of leaves. May see fine webbing on leaves and stems; may see mites moving on leaf undersides; leaves become discolored and speckled, then turn brown and shrivel up.

What to Do: Wash off with strong spray of water daily until all signs of infestation are gone; predatory mites available through garden centers; spray plants with insecticidal soap or neem oil according to package directions.

Mosaic

see Viruses

Nematodes

Tiny worms that give plants disease symptoms. One type infects foliage and stems; the other infects roots. *Foliar:* yellow spots that turn brown on leaves; leaves shrivel and wither;

problem starts on lowest leaves and works up plant. *Root-knot:* plant is stunted; may wilt; yellow spots on leaves; roots have tiny bumps or knots. **What to Do:** Mulch soil; add organic matter; clean up debris in fall. Don't touch wet foliage of infected plants; can add parasitic nematodes to soil. Remove infected plants in extreme cases.

Rot

Several different fungi that affect different parts of the plant and can kill plant. *Crown rot:* affects base of plant, causing stems to blacken and fall over and leaves to yellow and wilt. *Root rot:* leaves yellow and plant wilts; digging up plant reveals roots rotted away. **What to Do:** Keep soil well drained; don't damage plant if you are digging around it; keep mulches away from plant base. Destroy infected plant if whole plant affected.

Rust

Fungi. Pale spots on upper leaf surfaces; orange, fuzzy or dusty spots on leaf undersides. Examples: blister rust, hollyhock rust. **What to Do:** Choose rust-resistant varieties; avoid handling wet leaves; provide good air circulation; clear up debris at end of season. Destroy infected plant parts. Spray with neem oil according to directions.

Scale Insects

Tiny, shelled insects that suck sap, weakening and possibly killing plant or making it vulnerable to other problems. Once female scale insect has pierced plant with mouthpart it is there for life. Juvenile scale insects are called crawlers.

What to Do: Wipe off with alcohol-soaked swabs; spray with water to dislodge crawlers; encourage natural predators and parasites; dispose of infected material carefully at end of summer.

Slugs & Snails

Both are mollusks; slugs lack shells whereas snails have spiral shells. Slimy, smooth skin; can be up to 8" long, many are smaller; gray, green, black, beige, yellow or spotted. Leave large, ragged holes in leaves and silvery slime trails on and around plants. **What to Do:** Attach strips of copper to wood around raised beds or to smaller boards inserted around susceptible groups of plants; slugs and snails will get shocked if they try to cross copper surfaces. Pick off by hand in the evening and squish with boot or drop in can of soapy water. Spread wood ash or diatomaceous earth (available at garden centers) on ground around plants; it will pierce their soft bodies and cause them to dehydrate. Slug baits containing iron phosphate are not harmful to humans or animals and control slugs very well when used according to package directions. If slugs damaged garden last season, begin controls as soon as new green shoots appear in spring.

Sooty Mold

Fungus. Thin black film forms on leaf surfaces and reduces amount of light getting to leaf surfaces. **What to Do:** Wipe mold off leaf surfaces; control insects like aphids, mealybugs, whiteflies (honeydew left on leaves encourages mold).

Thrips

Difficult to see; may be visible if you disturb them by blowing gently on an infested flower. Yellow, black or brown; tiny, slender; narrow fringed wings. Suck juice out of plant cells, particularly in flowers and buds, causing mottled petals and leaves, dying buds and distorted and stunted growth.
What to Do: Remove and destroy infected plant parts; encourage native predatory insects with nectar plants like yarrow; spray severe infestations with insecticidal soap or neem oil according to package directions.

Viruses

Plant may be stunted and leaves and flowers distorted, streaked or discolored. Viral diseases in plants cannot be treated. Examples: mosaic virus, ringspot virus.
What to Do: Control insects like aphids, leafhoppers and whiteflies that spread disease. Destroy infected plants.

Whiteflies

Tiny flying insects that flutter up into the air when plant is disturbed. Tiny, moth-like, white; live on undersides of plant leaves. Suck juice out of leaves, causing yellowed leaves and weakened plants; leave behind sticky honeydew on leaves, encouraging sooty mold.
What to Do: Destroy weeds where insects may live. Attract native predatory beetles and parasitic wasps with nectar plants like yarrow; spray severe cases with insecticidal soap. Can make a sticky flypaper-like trap by mounting tin can on stake; wrap can with yellow paper and cover with clear plastic bag smeared with petroleum jelly; replace baggie when covered in flies.

Ladybird beetles are beneficial garden predators.

Wilt

If watering hasn't helped a wilted plant, one of two wilt fungi may be at fault. *Fusarium* wilt: plant wilts, leaves turn yellow then die; symptoms generally appear first on one part of plant before spreading to other parts. *Verticillium* wilt: plant wilts; leaves curl up at edges; leaves turn yellow then drop off; plant may die.
What to Do: Both wilts difficult to control. Choose resistant plant varieties and cultivars; clean up debris at end of growing season. Destroy infected plants; solarize (sterilize) soil before re-planting (this may help if you've lost an entire bed of plants to these fungi)—contact local garden center for assistance.

Worms

see Caterpillars, Nematodes

About This Guide

THE ANNUALS IN THIS BOOK are organized alphabetically by their most familiar, local common names. Other common names and scientific names appear after the primary reference, and all names can be found in the index. The illustrated Flowers at a Glance section at the beginning of the book will familiarize you with the different flowers quickly, and it will help you find a plant if you aren't sure what it's called.

At the beginning of each entry in this book, you can find information on height, spread and flower color. At the back of the book, the Quick Reference Chart summarizes different features and requirements of the annuals; you will find this chart handy guide when planning for diversity in your garden.

For each annual, we give clear instructions for seeding, planting and growing, as well as useful tips for placing the plant around the garden. We also describe our favorite species, hybrids, cultivars and varieties. Note: Plant heights and spreads are given in the 'Recommended' section only if the values differ from the ranges at the beginning of the entry. Keep in mind, too, that many more types of each annual are often available; check with your local greenhouses or garden centers.

Common pests or diseases that may afflict a plant, if any, are also listed for each entry. The 'Problems & Pests' section in the book's introduction provides information on how to prevent and treat these problems.

Finally, note that where blooming times are mentioned, they refer to an average for Michigan. The last-frost date is specific to your area of the state; refer to the map on p. 13 and consult your local garden center.

The
Annuals
for Michigan

Abutilon
Flowering Maple, Chinese Lantern
Abutilon

Height: 18–36" **Spread:** 18–24" **Flower color:** red, pink, white, orange, yellow

THIS TENDER SHRUB, A POPULAR houseplant in the Victorian era, has taken to the garden thanks to new varieties with large flowers in sherbet shades of orange, yellow and pink. If brought indoors before frost, the plant will overwinter and flower almost all year round. Abutilon is best grown as a standard in a pot or as a companion plant in window boxes and large containers. Some varieties mature to a height of 5' if left unpruned.

This plant is in the mallow family and is not related to maples, as one of the common names suggests.

Planting

Seeding: Indoors in early winter with soil at 70°–75° F; blooms in 5–6 months from seed

Planting out: After last frost

Spacing: 24"

Growing

Abutilon grows well in **full sun** but can benefit from some shade during the afternoon. The soil should be **average to fertile, moist** and **well drained.** Pinch back growing tips to encourage bushy growth.

Tips

Include Abutilon in borders and mixed containers. Container-grown plants are easier to bring indoors for the winter. There they will continue to bloom for most of the fall and winter. Indoor plants will need a bright window and should be allowed to dry out between waterings in winter.

Recommended

A. x *hybridum* (*A. globosum*) is a bushy, mound-forming shrub that can be treated as an annual or wintered indoors and moved outside for the summer. Drooping, cup- or trumpet-shaped flowers are borne for most of the summer. Named varieties are available, but most seed catalogs sell seeds in mixed packets, so flower colors will be a surprise.

Problems & Pests

Few problems occur in the garden, but whiteflies, mealybugs and scale insects can cause trouble when plants are moved indoors.

Abutilon is one of the few plants that, depending on the climate, may be grown as an annual, a perennial or a shrub.

African Daisy
Monarch of the Veldt
Arctotis (Venidium)

Height: 12–24" **Spread:** 12–16" **Flower color:** pink, orange, yellow, red, white

IF YOU LOVE THE BRIGHT FACES OF DAISIES AND GLOWING COLORS to boot, African daisies are for you. And if you're looking for something really special, 'Zulu Prince' is worth growing from seed. The 2" wide, white, daisy-petaled blooms boast concentric inner rings of purple and yellow that highlight the elegant black centers. Easy to grow, African daisies thrive in heat and drought and make marvelous cut flowers. The flowers close at night and on overcast days, so site them in beds where they can be enjoyed during daylight hours.

Planting

Seeding: Indoors in early spring; direct sow after last frost

Planting out: Once soil has warmed

Spacing: 12–16"

Growing

Choose a location in **full sun**. The soil should be **average, moist** and **well drained**. African daisies don't mind sandy soil, and they tolerate drought well. Keep the plants deadheaded and they will flower continuously from mid-summer to frost.

Seeds started indoors should be planted in peat pots or peat pellets to avoid disturbing the roots when the seedlings are transplanted. African daisy seeds do not keep, so purchase or collect new seeds each year.

Tips

African daisies can be grouped or massed in beds, borders and cutting gardens. They do quite well when grown in planters and other containers. You can try growing a fall crop—sow seeds directly in the garden in mid-summer and enjoy the flowers all fall.

Recommended

A. fastuosa (Monarch of the Veldt, Cape Daisy) has bright orange flowers with a purple spot at the base of each petal. It grows 12–24" tall and spreads 12". '**Zulu Prince**' bears large cream white or yellow flowers with bands of brown or purple and orange or yellow at the base of each petal, surrounded by deeply lobed leaves of silvery white.

A. stoechadifolia var. *grandis* (African Daisy) has 3" wide, white blooms with a yellow ring, and the undersides of the petals are pale lavender blue. The plant has a nice bushy form and grows 24" tall and 16" wide.

Several hybrids feature striking flowers. **Harlequin Hybrids** grow up to 20" tall and spread 12" wide. They do not come true from seed and are propagated by cuttings. The flowers may be pink, red, white, orange or yellow.

Problems & Pests

Watch for aphids, leaf miners, downy mildew and leaf spot.

Ageratum
Floss Flower
Ageratum

Height: 6–36" **Spread:** 6–18" **Flower color:** white, pink, mauve, blue

WONDERFUL NEW VARIETIES OF AGERATUM HAVE GIVEN THIS OLD-fashioned favorite new life. Brilliant shades of blue, violet, dusty mauve rose and white make it a versatile choice for beds and borders as well as containers. Taller varieties that reach 2–3', such as 'Blue Horizon,' provide summer-long color in perennial gardens and make wonderful cut flowers. To create an old-fashioned border, mix blue Ageratum with pink begonias and white Alyssum. For a low-maintenance combo, try Dusty Miller mixed with blue Ageratum and lemon yellow marigolds. Add a few white petunias for a crisp look.

Planting

Seeding: Indoors in early spring; direct sow after last frost. Don't cover the seeds; they need light to germinate.

Planting out: Once soil has warmed

Spacing: About 4–12"

Growing

Ageratum prefers **full sun** but tolerates partial shade. The soil should be **fertile, moist** and **well drained**. This plant doesn't like to have its soil dry out; a moisture-retaining mulch will cut down on how frequently you have to water it. Don't mulch too thickly or too close to the base of the plant or it may develop crown rot or root rot.

Though the plant needs deadheading to keep it flowering, the blossoms are extraordinarily long-lived, making Ageratum an easy-care plant for sunny gardens.

When cut fresh in the morning, Ageratum plants can be bundled together with rubber bands, hung upside down in a location with good air circulation and used for crafts and dried floral arrangements.

'Blue Hawaii' (below)

'Blue Hawaii' (this page)

Tips

The smaller varieties, which become almost completely covered with the fluffy flowerheads, make excellent edging plants for flowerbeds. They are also attractive grouped in masses or grown in planters. The taller varieties are useful in the center of a flowerbed and make interesting cut flowers.

The original species is a tall, leggy plant that was not considered attractive enough for the annual border but was used in the cutting garden. New cultivars are much more compact, and Ageratum is now a proudly displayed annual.

The genus name, Ageratum, *is derived from Greek and means 'without age,' a reference to the long-lasting flowers.*

Recommended

A. houstonianum forms a large, leggy mound that can grow up to 24" tall. Clusters of fuzzy blue, white or pink flowers are held above the foliage. Many cultivars are available; most have been developed to maintain a low, compact form that is more useful in the border. **'Bavaria'** grows about 10" tall with blue and white bicolored flowers. **'Blue Hawaii'** is a compact plant 6–8" tall, with blue flowers. **'Blue Horizon'** is an upright cultivar with lavender blue flowers. It grows 24–36" tall. **'Pinky Improved'** is a compact plant with subtle, dusky pink flowers. **'Summer Snow'** has white flowers.

Problems & Pests

Powdery mildew may become a problem. Be sure to plant Ageratum in a location with good air circulation to help prevent fungal diseases.

A. houstonianum (above), 'Blue Horizon' (below)

Agrostemma
Corn Cockle
Agrostemma

Height: 24–36" **Spread:** 12" **Flower color:** purple, pink, white

THIS PLANT IS KNOWN AS CORN COCKLE IN ENGLAND, WHERE IT IS often considered a weed because of its ability to re-seed. Agrostemma is rarely available as a transplant so it must be grown from seed. The simple but charming, pink, plum or white flowers are perched on the ends of long, skinny stems and are fun to use in wild cottage gardens and other relaxed plantings. Seed Agrostemma directly in the garden, interspersed among tall fall bloomers, for soft color.

Planting

Seeding: Direct sow around last frost date or start indoors about a month earlier

Planting out: After last frost

Spacing: 8–12"

Growing

Agrostemma grows best in **full sun.** The soil should be of **poor fertility** and **well drained.** This plant prefers cool weather and may stop flowering during the hottest part of summer. Insert twiggy stakes around young plants to provide support as they grow. Deadhead to prolong blooming and prevent profuse self-seeding.

Tips

Agrostemma makes a good companion plant for bushy, silver-leaved perennials such as artemisias. The bright flowers stand out against the gray, and the stiffer perennial will support the weaker-stemmed annual. Agrostemma also makes a good filler plant for the middle of the border.

A. githago (above), 'Milas' (below)

If you have a cutting garden, add Agrostemma to the mix. Fresh cuts harvested just as the flowers open will last five days or more in a floral arrangement.

The seeds can cause stomachaches if ingested.

Recommended

*A. **githago*** is an upright plant with gray-green leaves and purple or white flowers. '**Milas**' bears dark pink flowers.

Problems & Pests

Rare problems with leaf spot are possible.

Alyssum
Sweet Alyssum
Lobularia

Height: 3–12" **Spread:** 6–24" **Flower color:** pink, purple, yellow, salmon, white, bicolored

A LARGE, LACY MOUND OF ALYSSUM PLANTED NEAR THE KITCHEN door will greet all who enter with a honey-sweet fragrance during the growing season. When used as an edger in planters, the mounds of thimble-shaped flower clusters will spill over the edges like free-flowing frosting. Should it swoon during the dog days of August, when night temperatures remain high, shear back the frazzled plants to encourage a fresh flush of blooms when temperatures come down in fall. Alyssum's ability to handle a light frost makes it a good choice for those who like to push the envelope in late-season planting.

Planting

Seeding: Indoors in late winter; direct sow in spring

Planting out: Once soil has warmed

Spacing: 8–12"

Growing

Alyssum prefers **full sun** but tolerates light shade. **Well-drained** soil with **average fertility** is preferred, but poor soil is tolerated. This plant dislikes having its roots disturbed, so if starting it indoors, use peat pots or pellets. Trim Alyssum back occasionally over the summer to keep it flowering and looking good.

Leave Alyssum plants out all winter. In spring, remove the previous year's growth to expose self-sowed seedlings below.

L. maritima (this page)

Tips

Alyssum will creep around rock gardens, on rock walls and along the edges of beds. It is an excellent choice for seeding into cracks and crevices of walkway and patio stones, and once established it readily reseeds. It is also good for filling in spaces between taller plants in borders and mixed containers.

Alyssum, *the original genus name for this annual, comes from the Greek and means 'not madness,' referring to the belief that the plant could cure rabies.*

Recommended

L. maritima forms a low, spreading mound of foliage. The entire plant appears to be covered in tiny blossoms when it is in full flower. 'Pastel Carpet' bears flowers in rose, white, violet and mauve. 'Snow Crystal' bears large, bright white flowers profusely all summer. 'Wonderland' series offers a mix of all colors on compact plants.

Problems & Pests

Alyssum rarely has problems but is sometimes afflicted with downy mildew.

Amaranthus
Amaranth
Amaranthus

Height: 3–5' **Spread:** 12–30" **Flower color:** red, yellow, green; flowers inconspicuous in some species grown for foliage

WHETHER YOU CHOOSE THE GRACEFUL draping plumes of Love-lies-bleeding or the neon, feather-duster-like foliage of Joseph's Coat, Amaranthus species are sure to become conversation pieces in your garden. Joseph's Coat is especially attractive when viewed from above, so consider using it in beds that are viewed from second-story windows or elevated decks. Love-lies-bleeding makes an interesting addition to fresh or dried flower arrangements. There are many other interesting varieties of amaranthus to choose from as well, so be sure to check them out at your local garden center.

Planting

Seeding: Indoors about three weeks before last frost; direct sow once soil has warmed

Planting out: Once soil has warmed

Spacing: 12–24"

Growing

A location in **full sun** is preferable. The soil should be **poor to average** and **well drained**. Don't give these plants rich soil or overfertilize them, or their growth will be tall, soft and prone to falling over. Joseph's Coat will also lose some of its leaf color when overfertilized; its colors will be more brilliant in poorer soil.

Seeds started indoors should be planted in peat pots or pellets to avoid disturbing the roots when transplanting them.

Love-lies-bleeding self-seeds and can show up year after year. Any unwanted plants are easy to uproot when they are young.

A. caudatus (above), cultivar (below)

A. *caudatus* cultivars (this page)

Tips

Love-lies-bleeding is attractive grouped in borders or in mixed containers, where it requires very little care or water over summer. Joseph's Coat is a bright and striking plant that is best used as an annual specimen plant in a small group rather than in a large mass planting, where it quickly becomes overwhelming. It is also attractive mixed with large foliage plants in the back of a border.

Recommended

A. caudatus (Love-lies-bleeding) has erect stems and long, drooping, rope-like, fluffy red, yellow or green flower spikes that can be air dried. The plant grows 3–5' tall and 18–30" wide.

In ancient Greece, amaranthus was regarded as a symbol of constancy and fidelity.

A. tricolor (Joseph's Coat) is a bushy, upright plant with brightly colored foliage. It grows up to 5' tall and spreads 12–24". The foliage is variegated and can be green, red, bronze, chocolaty purple, orange, yellow or gold. '**Illumination**' has hanging foliage in crimson and gold and inconspicuous flowers. It grows 4' tall and 12" wide.

Problems & Pests

Cold nights below 50° F will cause leaf drop. Rust, leaf spot, root rot, aphids and some viral diseases are potential problems.

Several species of amaranthus are used as vegetables and potherbs because the leaves are high in protein; other species are grown as cereal crops.

A. t. 'Illumination' (above), A. tricolor (below)

Angel's Trumpet
Datura, Trumpet Flower
Datura, Brugmansia

Height: 3–10' **Spread:** 3–5' **Flower color:** white, yellow, purple

ANGEL'S TRUMPETS ARE PRIZED FOR their large, showy, trumpet-shaped flowers, which emit a lovely fragrance in the evening garden. These tender perennials easily over-winter indoors. Before threat of frost, bring them indoors to a bright, cool location. They can be grown as houseplants and may flower for much of the winter, or they can be cut back hard and overwintered in a cool, dark room such as a basement. All parts of these beautiful plants are poisonous, so if you have small children or plant-eating puppies, wait to grow any Datura species until they grow up.

Planting

Seeding: Slow to germinate. Start indoors in mid-winter. May not grow to flowering size until late summer.

Planting out: Once soil has warmed and frost danger has passed

Spacing: 24–36"

Growing

Angel's trumpets prefer **full sun.** The soil should be **fertile, moist** and **well drained.** Water sparingly, just enough to keep the soil from drying out. Don't allow plants to completely dry out, particularly during hot, dry weather. Plants recover quickly from wilting when watered.

B. candida cultivar (above),
D. x *h.* 'Angel's Trumpets' (below)

Propagate seeds indoors in early or mid-winter. Have patience because the seeds can be slow to germinate. Keep the soil moist but not soggy. The popularity of these plants has been increasing in recent years, and many garden centers carry started plants.

Tips

Angel's trumpet flowers tend to open at night. Grow these plants where you will be able to enjoy their intoxicating scent in the evening— near a patio or in a large container on a deck. If angel's trumpets are planted under an open window, the scent will carry into the room. These plants are attractive used as specimens or in groups.

Recommended

These plants may be attributed to the genus *Datura* or *Brugmansia.* The two genera are closely related.

In general, herbaceous annuals and perennials with upright flowers are classified as *Datura* while the woody plants with pendulous flowers are classified as *Brugmansia*. This rule of thumb is only slightly helpful because many of the woody plants are treated as tender annuals or perennials, and many catalogs and garden centers have the plants named incorrectly. Don't worry too much about the names; if you find a plant you like, go ahead and try it.

***B. aurea** (D. aurea)* is a woody plant that can be grown indoors in a cool, bright room in winter and outdoors in summer. When grown outdoors, it bears bright yellow or white, scented flowers all summer. In the tropics this plant may grow as tall as 30', but in a container or border it will rarely grow taller than 5'. Growth can be controlled by trimming.

D. x h. 'Purple Queen' (above), B. aurea (below)

B. candida is a woody plant that can be grown in a bright room indoors in winter and moved outdoors in summer. In a container it rarely grows over 10'. Trim it back to keep it the size you want. It bears fragrant, white, trumpet-shaped flowers that may open only at night. 'Grand Marnier' has apricot yellow flowers.

B. 'Charles Grimaldi' is another woody plant. The large, funnel-shaped, pendulous flowers are lemon yellow. This is an excellent container plant for a patio or deck.

D. x *hybrida* (*B.* x *hybrida*) includes several hybrid plants of uncertain parentage. 'Angel's Trumpets' ('Angel') bears white flowers edged with pale pink. The hybrids in the 'Queen' series are commonly available, often offered in seed catalogs.

'Golden Queen' has yellow double flowers. 'Purple Queen' has double flowers; the inner petals are white and the outer petals are purple.

D. innoxia (*D. meteloides*) is a small tender perennial grown as an annual. It grows 3'. The flowers are white, pink or lavender.

Problems & Pests

Problems with whiteflies, spider mites and mealybugs are possible, though more likely on plants grown indoors.

*Angel's trumpets are in the same family as tomatoes, potatoes, peppers and nightshade plants. As are many of its cousins, angel's trumpets are **poisonous** and people have died from eating them, particularly the seeds.*

Angel Wings

Angelonia

Height: 12–24" **Spread:** 12" **Flower color:** purple, white

THIS RELATIVELY NEW INTRODUCTION TO American gardens promises to be a real winner. In my garden, both the purple and bicolored purple and white varieties produced season-long color in spite of intense heat and drought. Dainty, orchid-like blossoms cover the 24" tall, shrub-like plants throughout the growing season. Removing spent stems to keep the plant tidy and watering when the soil begins to dry are about all you need to do to Angel Wings, making it an easy-care winner for beds, borders and containers. The white version, 'Alba,' seems somewhat less hardy than the purple varieties.

Planting

Seeding: Not recommended

Planting out: In warm soil after last frost

Spacing: 8–12"

The individual flowers look a bit like orchid blossoms, but Angel Wings is actually in the same family as snapdragons.

Growing

Angel Wings prefers **full sun** but tolerates a bit of shade. The soil should be **fertile, moist** and **well drained**. Though this plant grows naturally in damp areas, such as along ditches and near ponds, it is fairly drought tolerant.

This plant is not worth trying to save from year to year because it tends to lose its attractive habit as it matures. Cuttings can be taken in late summer and grown indoors over the winter to be used the following summer.

Tips

With its loose, airy spikes of orchid-like flowers, Angel Wings makes a welcome addition to the annual or mixed border. Include it in a pond-side or streamside planting or in a mixed planter.

A. angustifolia (above), 'Alba' (below)

Recommended

A. angustifolia is a perennial that is treated like an annual. It is a bushy, upright plant with loose spikes of flowers in varied shades of purple. 'Alba' bears white flowers. 'Blue Pacific' bears bicolored flowers of white and purple.

Problems & Pests

Aphids and powdery mildew can cause trouble.

Baby's Breath
Gypsophila

Height: 12–36" **Spread:** 12–24" **Flower color:** white, pink, mauve

THE DELICATE, FROTHY FLOWERS OF BABY'S BREATH HAVE LONG been valued as a filler for cut-flower arrangements. In similar style, the plant makes a charming companion in the cottage garden, calming down the magentas and oranges and filling gaps between blooms. When grown from seed it will flower in just six to eight weeks, but because this annual is short-lived, sow additional seeds every two weeks for a season-long show. Annual Baby's Breath is a nice alternative for those averse to the invasive perennial version.

Planting

Seeding: Indoors in late winter; direct sow from mid-spring to early summer

Planting out: Mid-spring

Spacing: 8–18"

Growing

Baby's Breath grows best in **full sun.** The soil should be of **poor fertility,** and it should be **light, sandy** and **alkaline.** This plant is drought tolerant; take care not to overwater because it does not grow well in wet soil. Don't space the seedlings too far apart because slightly crowded plants flower more profusely. Individual plants are short-lived, so sow seeds every week or two until early summer to encourage a longer blooming period.

Tips

The clouds of flowers are ideal for rock gardens, rock walls, mixed containers or borders with bold-colored flowers. Native to the northeastern Mediterranean, Baby's Breath looks very good in a Mediterranean-style garden.

Recommended

G. elegans forms an upright mound of airy stems, foliage and flowers. The plant grows 12–24" tall. The flowers are usually white but may have pink or purple veining that gives the flowers a colored tinge. 'Covent Garden' has very large, white flowers and grows to 20–36" tall. 'Gypsy Pink' bears double or semi-double pink flowers. This compact cultivar grows about 12" tall.

G. elegans (this page)

Problems & Pests

Most of the more common problems are fungal diseases that can be avoided by not overwatering and not handling plants when they are wet. Leafhoppers can infect plants with aster yellows.

Gypsophila comes from the words gypsum, or sulfate of lime, and philos, 'loving,' referring to the plant's preference for chalky soils.

Bachelor's Buttons
Cornflower, Blue-Bottle
Centaurea

Height: 12–39" **Spread:** 6–24" **Flower color:** blue, violet, red, pink, white

THIS OLD-TIME FAVORITE IS ENJOYING RENEWED POPULARITY thanks to the trends in wild and cottage gardens. The long-lasting flowers in blue, rose, violet and white are borne atop thin, wiry stems and make wonderful additions to cut-flower arrangements. To keep these short-lived charmers blooming, start the season with transplants and seeds, then sow additional seeds every couple of weeks throughout the summer to replace the earlier plants as they fade.

Planting

Seeding: Direct sow in mid-spring or start indoors in late winter

Planting out: Around last frost

Spacing: 12"

A bachelor's button is a button with a wire attached to the back. It doesn't need to be sewn on to stay attached to a shirt. Perhaps these flowers were once used for the same purpose.

Growing

Bachelor's Buttons will do best in **full sun. Fertile, moist, well-drained** soil is preferable, but any soil is tolerated. Light frost won't harm the plants.

Seed started indoors should be planted in peat pots or pellets to avoid disturbing roots during transplanting. Shear spent flowers and old foliage in mid-summer for fresh new growth. Deadheading prolongs blooming.

C. cyanus (this page)

The scientific name means 'century' and refers to the folklore that this plant can live for a hundred years; it re-seeds easily and quickly outgrows most pest problems.

Tips

Bachelor's Buttons is a great filler plant in a mixed border or wildflower or cottage-style garden. It is attractive when used in masses or small groups. Mix it with other plants—as the Bachelor's Buttons fades, the other plants can fill in the space it leaves.

Recommended

C. cyanus is an upright annual that grows 12–36" tall and spreads 6–24". The flowers of this plant are most often blue but can be in shades of red, pink, violet or white. Plants in the '**Boy**' series grow up to 39" tall and have large double flowers in many colors. '**Florence**' is a compact, dwarf cultivar that grows 12–18" tall and has flowers in various colors. '**Polka Dot**' bears flowers in shades of blue, purple, red, pink and white on plants that grow about 18" tall.

Problems & Pests

Aphids, downy mildew and powdery mildew may cause problems.

Bacopa

Sutera

Height: 3–6" **Spread:** 12–20" **Flower color:** white, lavender

WHO WOULDN'T FALL IN LOVE WITH A PLANT THAT PRODUCES AN elegant curtain of tiny, green leaves showered with delicate, white, star-shaped flowers? As an edging filler for containers, Bacopa gets rave reviews. Because it resents the heat of summer, it is best used in containers and window boxes that are protected from the hot afternoon sun or that can be moved to a shaded area when the weather heats up. It is imperative that soil in the container not be allowed to dry out. As many a sad gardener has discovered, a dry Bacopa is a dead Bacopa.

Bacopa is a perennial that is grown as an annual outdoors. It will thrive as a houseplant in a bright room.

Planting

Seeding: Not recommended

Planting out: Once soil has warmed

Spacing: 12"

Growing

Bacopa grows well in **partial shade,** with protection from the hot afternoon sun. The soil should be of **average fertility, humus rich, moist** and **well drained.** Don't allow this plant to completely dry out; the leaves will die quickly if they become dry. Cutting back the dead growth may encourage new shoots to form.

'Giant Snowflake' (above),
S. cordata and Geranium (below)

Tips

Bacopa is a popular plant for hanging baskets, mixed containers and window boxes. It is not recommended as a bedding plant because it fizzles quickly when the weather gets hot, particularly if you forget to water.

Recommended

S. cordata is a compact, trailing plant that bears small, white flowers all summer. **'Giant Snowflake'** is a more vigorous development of 'Snowflake.' **'Lavender Showers'** forms a dense mound of heart-shaped leaves with scalloped edges and bears tiny, star-shaped, lavender flowers along its neat, trailing stems. **'Olympic Gold'** has gold-variegated foliage with white flowers. **'Snowflake,'** one of the first cultivars available, bears white flowers.

Problems & Pests

Whiteflies and other small insects can become a real menace to this plant because the tiny leaves and dense growth are perfect hiding spots for them.

Begonia
Begonia

Height: 6–24" **Spread:** 6–24" **Flower color:** pink, white, red, yellow, orange, bicolored or picotee; plant also grown for foliage

TUBEROUS BEGONIAS ARE THE STARS OF THE SHADE GARDEN SET, and whether used in containers or beds, the 'Non-stop' series takes center stage. Covered with bunches of brilliant, half-dollar-sized blossoms, they never fail to get attention. Bedding or wax begonias are excellent choices for mass plantings. In the past these begonias have been relegated to the shade garden, but when grown in the sun they produce larger plants with brighter blooms. 'Escargot' rex begonia combined with 'Wizard' series Coleus and 'Elfin' series impatiens will light up any shaded corner.

Planting

Seeding: Indoors in early winter

Planting out: Once soil has warmed

Spacing: According to spread of variety

Growing

Light or partial shade is best, although some of the wax begonias tolerate sun if their soil is kept moist. The soil should be **fertile,** rich in **organic matter** and **well drained** with a **neutral or acidic** pH. Allow the soil to dry out slightly between waterings, particularly for tuberous begonias. Begonias are warm weather lovers, so don't plant them before the soil warms in spring. If they sit in cold soil, they may become stunted and fail to thrive.

B. semperflorens (above)

Begonias can be tricky to grow from seed. The tiny seeds can be mixed with a small quantity of fine sand before sowing to ensure a more even distribution of seeds. Keep the soil surface moist but not soggy, do not cover the seeds, and maintain daytime temperatures at 70°–80° F and night temperatures above 50° F. Begonias can be potted individually once they have three or four leaves and are large enough to handle.

Tubers can be purchased in early spring and started indoors. Plant them with the concave side up. The tubers of tuberous begonias can also be uprooted when the foliage dies back and stored in slightly moistened peat moss over winter. The tuber will sprout new shoots in late winter and can be potted for the following season.

Wax begonias can be dug out of the garden before the first frost and grown as houseplants in winter in a bright room.

B. *semperflorens* cultivar (above),
B. Rex Cultorum hybrid 'Escargot' (below)

Tips

All begonias are useful for shaded garden beds and planters. The trailing tuberous varieties can be used in hanging baskets and along rock walls where the flowers will cascade over the edges. Wax begonias have a neat rounded habit that makes them particularly attractive as edging plants. They can also be paired with roses and geraniums in a front-yard bed for a formal look. Creative gardeners are using the begonias with dramatic foliage as specimen plants in containers and beds.

Recommended

B. Rex Cultorum Hybrids (rex begonias) are a group of plants developed from crosses between *B. rex* and other species. They are grown for their dramatic, colorful foliage. These plants can also be grown as houseplants, and in that form the leaves take on different colors depending on the levels of light. 'Colorvision' is available from seed and provides plants with pink, red, bronze and white markings on green leaves. 'Escargot' has brightly colored leaves that form an unusual spiral shape.

B. semperflorens (wax begonias) have pink, white, red or bicolored flowers and green, bronze, reddish or white-variegated foliage. The plants are 6–14" tall and 6–24" wide. Plants in the 'Ambassador' series are heat tolerant and have dark green leaves and white, pink or red flowers. 'Cocktail' series plants are sun and heat tolerant and have bronzed leaves and red, pink or white flowers.

B. x *tuberhybrida* (tuberous begonias) are generally sold as tubers.
The flowers come in shades of red,
pink, yellow, orange or white. They
can also be picotee, with the petal
margins colored differently than the
rest of the petal. The plants are 8–24"
tall and wide. '**Non-stop**' series
begonias can be started from seed.
The plants grow about 12" both tall
and wide; their double and semi-
double flowers come in pink, yellow,
orange, red and white. *B.* x *t. pendula*
'**Chanson**' includes attractive pendulous begonias with flowers in
many bright shades.

Problems & Pests

Problems with stem rot and gray
mold can occur from overwatering.

B. semperflorens and *Buxus* hedge (above),
B. x *tuberhybrida* (below)

Bells-of-Ireland
Moluccella

Height: 24–36"   **Spread:** 10"   **Flower color:** green

A LOVELY CUT FLOWER, A DECORATIVE DRIED FLORAL AND AN interesting addition to a mixed border or cottage-style planting, the versatile Bells-of-Ireland deserves to be used in more Michigan gardens. Occasionally found as a transplant in garden centers, the plant is easily grown from seed sowed directly in the garden after all chance of frost is past. To use Bells-of-Ireland in fresh flower arrangements, cut the stems when three-quarters of the green whorls are open. For dried arrangements, harvest when all the flowers are open, and hang them upside down to dry.

Planting

Seeding: Indoors in mid-winter or direct sow in mid-spring

Planting out: After last frost

Spacing: 12"

Growing

Bells-of-Ireland prefers to grow in **full sun** but tolerates partial shade. The soil should be of **average or good fertility, moist** and **well drained**.

Newly planted seeds need light to germinate. Press them into the soil surface, but leave them uncovered. Sow directly into the garden because these plants resent being transplanted.

The tall stems may need staking in windy locations.

Tips

Use Bells-of-Ireland at the back of a border, where the green spikes will create an interesting backdrop for more brightly colored flowers.

This plant is prone to self-seeding.

Recommended

M. laevis is an upright plant that bears spikes of creamy white, inconspicuous flowers. The interesting feature of the plant is the large, green, shell-like cup that encircles each flower. The species is generally grown and cultivars are rarely offered.

Contrary to what the name implies, these plants are native to the Middle East, not to Ireland.

These plants are popular in fresh or dried flower arrangements. When dried, the green cups become white or beige and papery.

Bidens

Bidens

Height: 12–24" **Spread:** 12–24" or more **Flower color:** yellow

THE TRAILING HABIT OF BIDENS MAKES IT A PERFECT PLANT TO use as an edging in beds bordered by cement or paving bricks. The fern-like foliage with pretty little golden flowers spills onto the concrete, softening the lines like a lovely ruffled collar. And this tough little character can take the heat that would turn less hardy plants to toast. Bidens can be used as an edger or filler in beds and containers and looks attractive when accented with flashy annuals such as purple 'Fantasy' petunias.

This species of Bidens is native to the southern U.S. and Mexico, so it is well equipped to handle full sun and heat in your garden.

Planting

Seeding: Direct sow in late spring or start indoors in late winter

Planting out: After last frost

Spacing: 12–24"

Growing

Bidens grows well in **full sun.** The soil should be **average to fertile, moist** and **well drained.**

If plants become lank and unruly in summer, shear them back lightly to encourage new growth and fall flowers.

Tips

Bidens can be included in mixed borders, containers, hanging baskets and window boxes. Its fine foliage and attractive flowers makes it useful for filling spaces between other plants.

Recommended

B. ferulifolia is a bushy, mounding plant with ferny foliage and bright yellow flowers. **'Golden Goddess'** has even narrower foliage and larger flowers.

Problems & Pests

Problems can occur with fungal diseases such as leaf spot, powdery mildew and rust.

This cheerful plant in the daisy family is always in flower and makes a wonderful annual groundcover.

B. ferulifolia (this page), with *Calibrachoa* (below)

Black-Eyed Susan
Coneflower
Rudbeckia

Height: 8–36" or more **Spread:** 12–18" **Flower color:** yellow, orange, red, brown or sometimes bicolored; brown or green centers

ALTHOUGH IT IS ALSO SOLD AS A PERENNIAL, THIS BLACK-EYED Susan is marginally hardy in Michigan and is best grown as an annual. The large single or double flowers, in eye-catching shades of orange and gold with dark centers, demand attention wherever they grow. And because the flowers make a wonderful addition to fresh arrangements, deadheading to prolong the bloom should not be much of a chore. The green-centered 'Irish Eyes' is a good choice if you want bright color but less contrast. 'Irish Eyes' planted with Bells-of-Ireland, white nicotiana and bronze fennel makes an interesting combination of color and texture.

Black-eyed Susan is a bright-flowered native plant that makes an excellent addition to wildflower and natural gardens.

Planting

Seeding: Indoors in late winter; direct sow in mid-spring

Planting out: Late spring

Spacing: 18"

Growing

Black-eyed Susan grows equally well in **full sun** or **partial shade**. The soil should be of **average fertility, humus rich, moist** and **well drained**. This plant tolerates heavy clay soil and hot weather. If it is growing in loose, moist soil, Black-eyed Susan may re-seed itself.

Tips

Black-eyed Susan can be planted individually or in groups. Use it in beds and borders, large containers, meadow plantings and wildflower gardens. This plant will bloom well, even in the hottest part of the garden.

Keep cutting the flowers to promote more blooming. Black-eyed Susan makes a long-lasting vase flower.

R. hirta (above), 'Becky' (below)

R. hirta is a perennial that is grown as an annual. It is not worth trying to keep over winter because it grows and flowers quickly from seed.

Recommended

R. *hirta* forms a bristly mound of foliage and bears bright yellow, daisy-like flowers with brown centers in summer and fall. '**Becky**' is a dwarf cultivar up to 12" tall, with large flowers in solid and mixed shades of yellow, orange, red and brown. '**Cherokee Sunset**' bears 3–4^1/$_2$" semi-double and double flowers in all colors. It is an All-America winner for 2002.

This tough flower has long-lasting blooms that keep fall flowerbeds bright.

R. hirta (this page)

'Indian Summer' has huge flowers, 6–10" across, on sturdy stems 36" tall or taller. 'Irish Eyes' grows up to 30" tall and has green-centered single flowers. 'Toto' is a dwarf cultivar that grows 8–12" tall, small enough for planters.

Problems & Pests

Good air circulation around Black-eyed Susan plants will help prevent fungal diseases such as powdery mildew, downy mildew and rust. Aphids can also cause problems occasionally.

'Irish Eyes' (above), 'Cherokee Sunset' (below)

With its hairy stems that are difficult for insects to climb, Black-eyed Susan can act as a 'bug guard' near fields or houses.

Black-Eyed Susan Vine

Thunbergia

Height: 5' or more **Spread:** equal to height, if trained
Flower color: yellow, orange, violet blue or white, usually with dark centers

WHETHER IT'S THEIR SIMPLE SHAPE OR THEIR SOFT YELLOW-ORANGE color accented with a dark center, the flowers of these perky plants always make me smile. Grown in a container or window box, black-eyed Susan vines readily train to form a colorful frame around a window or doorway. Somewhat rare, but worth searching out, is the lovely *Thunbergia grandiflora*, which produces gorgeous, blue, trumpet-shaped flowers in late summer and fall.

Planting

Seeding: Indoors in mid-winter; direct sow in mid-spring

Planting out: Late spring

Spacing: 12–18"

Growing

Black-eyed Susan vines grow well in **full sun, partial shade** or **light shade.** Grow in **fertile, moist, well-drained** soil that is high in **organic matter.**

Tips

Black-eyed Susan vines can be trained to twine up and around fences, walls, trees and shrubs. They are also attractive trailing down from the top of a rock garden or rock wall or growing in mixed containers and hanging baskets.

These vines are perennials treated as an annuals. They can be quite vigorous and may need to be trimmed back from time to time, particularly if they are brought inside for winter. To acclimatize the plants to the lower light levels indoors, gradually move them to more shaded locations. Keep in a bright room out of direct sunlight for winter. The following spring, harden off the plants before moving them outdoors.

Recommended

T. alata is a vigorous, twining climber It bears yellow flowers, often with dark centers, in summer and fall. **'Susic'** is a commonly found series that bears large flowers in yellow, orange or white.

T. grandiflora (Skyflower Vine, Blue Trumpet Vine) is a less commonly available species than *T. alata;* it is most often found growing in greenhouses in our northern climate. It is also a twining climber but bears stunning, pale violet blue flowers. **'Alba'** has white flowers.

T. alata cultivars (this page)

Black-eyed Susan vine makes an excellent hanging plant. The blooms are trumpet shaped, with the dark centers forming a tube.

Blanket Flower
Gaillardia

Height: 12–36" **Spread:** 12–24" **Flower color:** red, orange or yellow, often in combination

THIS COLORFUL SOUTHWESTERN NATIVE MAKES AN ATTRACTIVE addition to large rockeries and berms, where the soil is not rich and good drainage is guaranteed. Prompt deadheading will discourage fungal disease in humid weather and keep the plants flowering right through frost. 'Red Plume,' the best of the cultivated varieties, was a 1991 All-America winner.

Planting

Seeding: Indoors in late winter; direct sow in mid-spring

Planting out: Mid- to late spring

Spacing: 12"

Growing

Blanket Flower prefers **full sun**. The soil should be of **poor or average fertility, light, sandy** and **well drained**. The less water this plant receives, the better it will do. Don't cover the seeds because they need light to germinate. They also require warm soil.

Deadhead to encourage more blooms.

Tips

Blanket Flower has an informal, sprawling habit that makes it a perfect addition to an casual cottage garden or mixed border. Because it is drought tolerant, it is well suited to exposed, sunny slopes, where it can help retain soil while more permanent plants are growing in.

Make sure to place Blanket Flower in a location where it will not get watered with other plants.

Recommended

G. pulchella forms a basal rosette of leaves. The daisy-like flowers are red with yellow tips. **'Plume'** series has double flowerheads in vibrant shades of red or yellow and includes the popular cultivar **'Red Plume.'** This dwarf plant grows about 12" tall, with an equal spread, and blooms for a long time.

Problems & Pests

Possible problems include leafhoppers, powdery mildew, aster yellows, rust and bacterial and fungal leaf spot. If you avoid overwatering, most problems will not become serious.

G. pulchella with *Echinops* (above)

Both the annual and the perennial Gaillardia *species are known for their plentiful, fire-bright blooms.*

This plant was named Blanket Flower because the vivid blossoms called to mind the colors in Navajo blankets.

Blue Lace Flower
Trachymene

Height: 24" **Spread:** 8–12" **Flower color:** lavender blue, white

BLUE LACE FLOWER IS A DAINTY RELATIVE OF QUEEN ANNE'S LACE but is far better behaved than its weedy cousin. Sowed directly into the garden after all danger of frost has passed, it is best grown in a cutting garden because it resents hot weather and does not flower when night temperatures rise above 70° F. A mid-summer sowing will provide you with fall-blooming plants, allowing you to take advantage of the cooler nights.

Planting

Seeding: Indoors in late winter; direct sow once soil has warmed

Planting out: After last frost

Spacing: 12"

Growing

Blue Lace Flower prefers a **sheltered location** in **full sun** that isn't too hot. It enjoys cool night temperatures. The soil should be of **average fertility, light** and **well drained.**

Sowing the seeds directly into the garden is preferable because the seedlings dislike having their roots disturbed. If you do start them indoors, sow the seeds in individual peat pots. The seeds can be slow to germinate.

Tips

Blue Lace Flower is used in beds and borders and is generally combined with other plants. The plants are quite erect, and with their delicate, feathery foliage they look good in an informal cottage-style garden. The flowers are long lasting when used in fresh arrangements.

Insert forked branches around young plants to keep them from flopping over in rain and wind.

Recommended

T. coerulea is a delicate, upright plant that bears light blue, scented flowers. 'Lace Veil' is a fragrant, white-flowered cultivar.

The genus name is from the Greek trachys, *'rough,' and* meninx, *'membrane,' referring to the fruit.*

T. coerulea (this page)

Blue Marguerite
Felicia, Blue Daisy
Felicia

Height: 10–24" **Spread:** 10–24" **Flower color:** many shades of blue or white with yellow centers

THE CHARMING, BLUE-PETALED, DAISY-LIKE FLOWERS OF THESE tender subshrubs add much-needed color to the late-summer and fall mixed perennial border. They also look fabulous tucked among the lavenders and thymes in herb beds. Though they will bloom all season, blue Marguerites pout when the temperatures soar. The good news is that, in my garden, they bounce back when things cool down and are not fazed by the first light frosts.

Planting

Seeding: Indoors in winter; direct sow in mid-summer

Planting out: After last frost

Spacing: 12"

Growing

Blue Marguerites like to grow in **full sun**. The soil should be of **average fertility** and **well drained**. These plants do not tolerate heat well. A mid-summer sowing will provide flowers in the cooler temperatures of fall. Take cuttings from the new fall growth of *F. amelloides* to start plants for the following spring. Taking cuttings will save you the uncertainty of starting with seeds or the trouble of trying to overwinter entire large plants.

Tips

Blue Marguerites, with their sprawling habits, are well suited to rock gardens, bed edges, mixed containers and hanging baskets. The flowers close at night and on cloudy days.

The key to keeping these plants looking their best is trimming. When they are young, pinch the tips to promote bushiness. Deadhead as the flowers fade, and cut the plants back when the flowering slows down during the heat of summer. They will revive in the cooler fall weather and produce a second flush of growth and more flowers.

Recommended

F. amelloides forms a rounded, bushy mound 12–24" in height and spread. It bears flowers of varied shades of blue all summer. This species is a perennial grown as an annual. 'Astrid Thomas' is a dwarf variety with medium blue flowers. It grows 10" tall, with an equal spread. 'Midnight' has deep blue flowers.

F. amelloides (this page)

F. heterophylla forms a low mat of grayish green foliage. It bears blue, daisy-like flowers all summer and grows 20–24" tall, with an equal spread.

Problems & Pests

Blue Marguerites are generally problem free, although aphids cause occasional trouble.

Browallia
Amethyst Flower
Browallia

Height: up to 8–18" **Spread:** up to 8–18" **Flower color:** purple, blue, white

IF YOUR FAVORITE COLOR IS BLUE AND YOUR GARDEN IS partially shaded or gets only morning sun, grow Browallia and you may fall in love. This lavender-flowered plant makes a delightful backdrop for pink or white *Impatiens* 'Elfin' and *Lobularia* 'Snow Crystal.' Browallia also makes a great container plant that can be grown indoors. Water moderately, keeping the soil just moist to the touch in winter, and feed with a low-nitrogen fertilizer once a month.

Planting
Seeding: Indoors in late winter

Planting out: Once soil has warmed

Spacing: 8–10"

Growing

Browallia tolerates any light conditions from full sun to full shade, but flower production and color are best in **partial shade**. The soil should be **fertile** and **well drained**. Do not cover the seeds when you plant them because they need light to germinate. They do not like the cold, so wait several weeks after the last frost before setting out the plants. Pinch tips often to encourage new growth and more blooms.

Tips

Grow Browallia in mixed borders, mixed containers or hanging baskets.

Browallia can be grown as a houseplant throughout the year or brought indoors at the end of the season to be used as a houseplant during winter.

Recommended

B. speciosa forms a bushy mound of foliage. This plant grows 8–18" tall with an equal or narrower spread and bears white, blue or purple flowers all summer. The **'Jingle Bells'** series includes **'Blue Bells'** and **'Silver Bells,'** which vary from 8" to 12" in both height and spread. **'Starlight'** forms a compact mound up to 8" high and wide. Its flowers may be light blue, bright blue, purple or white. The **'Troll'** series includes **'Blue Troll'** and **'White Troll,'** which are compact and bushy. They grow about 10" tall.

Problems & Pests

Browallia is generally problem free. Whiteflies may cause some trouble.

'White Troll' (above)

B. speciosa (center & below)

Calendula
Pot Marigold, English Marigold
Calendula

Height: 10–24" **Spread:** 8–20" **Flower color:** cream, yellow, gold, orange, apricot

THE CHEERY ORANGE, YELLOW AND GOLD FLOWERS OF CALENDULA add a warm ray of sunshine to a kitchen *potager,* a herb bed or a cottage garden. Add flash and dash to soups and salads by sprinkling them with the bright-colored, edible petals. Newer varieties include 'Pink Surprise,' which sports light orange to apricot flowers delicately tinged with pink. Check out the popular seed catalogs for taller, strong-stemmed cultivars that are grown for use as cut flowers.

Calendula flowers are popular kitchen herbs that can be added to stews for color or salads for flavoring. They can also be brewed into an infusion that is useful as a wash for minor cuts and bruises.

Planting

Seeding: Direct sow in mid-spring; sow indoors a month or so earlier

Planting out: Mid-spring

Spacing: 8–10"

Growing

Calendula does equally well in **full sun** or **partial shade**. It likes cool weather and can withstand a light frost. The soil should be of **average fertility** and **well drained**. Young plants are sometimes difficult to find in nurseries because Calendula is quick and easy to start from seed and that is how most gardeners grow it. A second sowing in mid-summer gives a good fall display. Deadhead to prolong blooming and keep plants looking neat.

C. officinalis cultivars (this page)

Tips

This informal plant looks attractive in borders and mixed into the vegetable patch. It can also be used in mixed planters. Calendula is a cold-hardy annual and often continues flowering until the ground freezes completely.

Recommended

C. officinalis is a vigorous, tough, upright plant 12–24" tall, with a slightly lesser spread. It bears daisy-like, single or double flowers in a wide range of yellow and orange shades. '**Bon Bon**' is a dwarf plant that grows 10–12" tall and comes in all available colors. '**Fiesta Gitana**' ('Gypsy Festival') is a dwarf plant that bears flowers in a wide range of colors. '**Pacific Beauty**' is a larger plant, growing about 18" tall. It bears large flowers in varied colors. '**Pink Surprise**' bears pale orange and apricot flowers tinged with pink.

Problems & Pests

Calendula plants are often trouble free, but they can have problems with aphids and whiteflies as well as powdery mildew and fungal leaf spot. They usually continue to perform well even when they are afflicted with such problems.

California Poppy
Eschscholzia

Height: 8–18" **Spread:** 8–18" **Flower color:** orange, yellow, red; less commonly pink, cream

TO ADD A DOSE OF SUNSHINE TO A WILDFLOWER GARDEN OR TO a sunny, well-drained slope, plant California Poppy. Regular deadheading is needed to keep a tidy look and extend the bloom, so if your time is short, plant in a relaxed setting where the poppies are viewed from a distance. For cut flowers, wait until the fluted buds are about to open, then pick the buds in the morning just after the dew has dried.

Planting
Seeding: Direct sow in early to mid-spring

Spacing: 6–12"

The petals of California Poppy are edible and will brighten up an everyday salad.

Growing

California Poppy prefers **full sun**. The soil should be of **poor or average fertility** and **well drained**. With too rich a soil, the growth will be lush and green but will bear few, if any, flowers. This plant is drought tolerant once established.

Never start this plant indoors because it dislikes having its roots disturbed. California Poppy will sprout quickly when planted directly in the garden. Sow in early spring for blooms in summer.

California Poppy requires a lot of water for germination and development of young plants. Until they flower, provide the plants with regular and frequent watering. Once they begin flowering, they are more drought tolerant.

Tips

California Poppy can be included in an annual border or annual planting in a cottage garden. This plant self-seeds wherever it is planted; it is perfect for naturalizing in a meadow garden or rock garden where it will come back year after year.

Recommended

E. californica forms a mound of delicate, feathery, blue-green foliage and bears satiny, orange or yellow flowers all summer. This plant grows 8–18". '**Ballerina**' has a mixture of colors and semi-double or double flowers. '**Chiffon**' forms compact plants, up to 8", that bear semi-double flowers in pink and apricot. '**Mission Bells**' bears ruffled, double and semi-double

E. californica (this page)

flowers in mixed and solid shades of orange, yellow, red, cream and pink. '**Thai Silk**' bears flowers in pink, red, yellow and orange with silky, wavy-edged petals. The compact plants grow 8–10" tall.

Problems & Pests

California Poppy generally has few pest problems, but fungi may cause trouble occasionally.

Candytuft
Iberis

Height: 6–12"   **Spread:** 8" or more   **Flower color:** white, pink, purple, red

YOU PROBABLY WON'T FIND THIS LITTLE-USED CHARMER IN THE form of transplants, but if you're looking for a perky little filler plant, Candytuft is easy to grow from seed. I first spied it when a neighbor planted it as an edger next to the sidewalk. The northern exposure received afternoon sun and, once established, the plants re-seeded themselves every year. In succeeding years, the variously colored blooms reverted to the dominant color of light pinkish lavender.

Planting

Seeding: Indoors in late winter; outdoors around last frost

Planting out: After last frost

Spacing: 6"

Growing

Candytuft prefers to grow in **full sun** or **partial shade**. The soil should be of **poor or average fertility, well drained** and have a **neutral or alkaline** pH.

I. umbellata (this page)

Deadheading when the seeds begin to form will keep Candytuft blooming, but do let some plants go to seed to guarantee repeat performances.

Tips

This informal plant can be used on rock walls, in mixed containers or as edging for beds.

Recommended

I. umbellata (Globe Candytuft) has flowers in shades of pink, purple, red or white. The plant grows 6–12" tall and spreads 8" or more. **'Dwarf Fairy'** ('Dwarf Fairyland') is a compact plant that bears many flowers in a variety of pastel shades.

Problems & Pests

Keep an eye open for slugs and snails. Caterpillars can also be a problem. In poorly drained soil, fungal problems may develop.

Trim Candytuft back lightly to promote new growth and more flowers.

Canterbury Bells
Cup-and-Saucer Plant
Campanula

Height: 18–36" **Spread:** 12" **Flower color:** blue, purple, pink, white

THIS SHOWY BIENNIAL IS A STAPLE IN THE TRADITIONAL ENGLISH cottage garden. First-year plants will form only basal foliage. If you start Canterbury Bells yourself from seed, plant seedlings in a holding bed, provide lots of protection the first winter and then transplant the following year to the place where it is to bloom. This plant has a good-sized taproot, so dig deep when transplanting. 'Russian Pink' is a true annual that will flower the first year if started in early spring.

Planting

Seeding: Indoors in mid-winter

Planting out: Early spring

Spacing: 6–12"

Growing

Canterbury Bells prefers **full sun** but tolerates partial shade. The soil should be **fertile, moist** and **well drained**. This plant will not suffer if the weather cools or if there is a light frost.

When sowing, leave seeds uncovered because they require light for germination. Harden off in a cold frame or on a sheltered porch before planting out. Canterbury Bells transplants easily, even when in full bloom.

Canterbury Bells is actually a biennial treated as an annual. This is why the plants must be started so early in the year. Small plants, those purchased in 3¹/₂" pots, are usually too small to grow to flowering size the first year.

The double flowers of this plant are referred to as 'hose in hose' because it looks like one flower is cupped inside another. Angel's trumpet and rhododendrons are other examples of plants with hose-in-hose flowers.

'Flora-Pleno' (above)

Tips

Planted in small groups, Canterbury Bells looks lovely in a border or rock garden. It also makes a good addition to a cottage garden or other informal garden where its habit of self-seeding can keep it popping up year after year. The tallest varieties produce good flowers for cutting. Use dwarf varieties in planters.

Recommended

C. medium forms a basal rosette of foliage. The pink, blue, white or purple cup-shaped flowers are borne on tall spikes. The plant grows 24–36" tall and spreads about 12". **'Bells of Holland'** is a dwarf cultivar about 18" tall. It has flowers in various colors. **'Champion'** is a true annual cultivar, flowering much sooner from seed than the species or many other cultivars. Blue or pink flowers are available. **'Flora-Pleno'** bears double flowers in all colors. **'Russian Pink'** is an heirloom plant that was recently re-introduced. It is another true annual cultivar. and it bears light pink flowers.

The common name derived from the Canterbury pilgrims who rode horses decorated with bells; the flowers were reminiscent of those bells.

Problems & Pests

Occasional, but infrequent, problems with aphids, crown rot, leaf spot, powdery mildew and rust are possible.

'Flora-Pleno' (above)

Cathedral Bells
Cup-and-Saucer Vine
Cobaea

Height: 6–25' or more **Spread:** equal to height, if trained
Flower color: green, maturing to purple or white

FIRST DISCOVERED IN MEXICO IN THE 1600s BY A JESUIT PRIEST, this fast-growing vine has flowers that will take your breath away. Although Cathedral Bells likes hot weather, warm nights will keep it from flowering, so you may have to be patient when we experience a long, hot summer. As the weather cools, it will burst into bloom, and the show is well worth the wait. This exuberant climber can reach 12–15' in a single season, so be sure to provide a sturdy trellis to support it.

Planting

Seeding: Indoors in mid-winter

Planting out: After last frost

Spacing: 12"

Growing

Cathedral Bells prefers **full sun**. It is fond of hot weather and will do best if planted in a sheltered site with southern exposure. The soil should be **moist, well drained** and of **average fertility**. Keep the vine well watered and avoid overfertilizing. Too much nitrogen causes it to grow vigorously but also delays flowering. Set the seeds on edge when planting them, and barely cover them with soil.

Tips

Grow Cathedral Bells up a trellis, over an arbor or along a chain-link fence. It requires a sturdy support in order to climb. It uses grabbing hooks to climb, so it won't be able to grow up a wall without something to grab. It can be trained to fill almost any space.

Recommended

C. scandens is a vigorous climbing vine from Mexico. Its flowers are creamy green when they open and mature to deep purple. **Var.** *alba* has white flowers.

Problems & Pests

This plant may have trouble with aphids.

This interesting vine has sweet-scented flowers that are a cream color with a green tinge when they open; the flowers darken to purple as they age.

A stiff wire trellis provides good support for Cathedral Bells.

China Aster

Callistephus

Height: 6–36" **Spread:** 10–18" **Flower color:** purple, blue, pink, red, white, peach, yellow

PRIZED FOR THEIR BEAUTY AS CUT FLOWERS, THE BLOOMS OF THIS old-fashioned favorite appear for only a few weeks, but oh, what a glorious show. Deadheading will not encourage re-blooming. By choosing different varieties, however, you can extend China Aster's season of bloom by several weeks. This shallow-rooted beauty must not be allowed to dry out, so use a light organic mulch to help keep the soil moist.

Planting

Seeding: Indoors in late winter; direct sow after last frost

Planting out: Once soil has warmed

Spacing: 6–12"

Growing

China Aster prefers **full sun** but will tolerate partial shade. The soil should be **fertile, evenly moist** and **well drained**. A pH that is **neutral or alkaline** is preferable.

This plant should be started in peat pots or peat pellets, because it doesn't like having its roots disturbed.

Tips

The flowers of China Aster put on a bright display when planted in groups. There are three height groups: dwarf, medium and tall. Use the dwarf and medium varieties as edging plants and the taller varieties for cut-flower arrangements. Tall varieties may require staking.

Recommended

C. chinensis is the parent of many varieties and cultivars. '**Comet**' is an early-flowering cultivar, growing about 10" tall, with large, quilled double flowers in white, yellow, pink, purple, red or blue. '**Duchess**' plants are wilt resistant. The sturdy stems, up to 24" tall, bear colorful flowers with petals that curve in towards the center. '**Meteor**' has plants up to 36" tall. The large flowers, up to 4" across, are bright red with yellow centers. '**Pot 'n' Patio**' is a popular dwarf cultivar that has double flowers and grows 6–8" tall, with an equal spread. '**Princess**' grows up to 24" tall and bears quilled, double or semi-double flowers in a wide range of colors.

C. chinensis (this page)

Problems & Pests

Wilt diseases and aster yellows can be prevented by planting China Aster in different locations each year and by planting resistant varieties. Keep China Aster away from Calendula, which hosts potentially harmful insects and diseases.

Chinese Forget-Me-Not

Cynoglossum

Height: 12–24" **Spread:** up to 12" **Flower color:** blue, sometimes pink or white

CONSIDER SEEDING CHINESE FORGET-ME-NOT IN THE MIDDLE OR at the back of the border. It will weave its way through tall perennial plantings and, like magic, cover the less than stellar foliage often found there. The shower of tiny blue flowers borne atop 24" stems will also make a lovely addition to cut-flower arrangements. Full sun and fast-draining soils are needed to keep this plant happy, and it will decline when summer heats up and humidity is on the rise. Make a second sowing in mid- to late summer for another show when the weather cools down in fall.

Planting

Seeding: Indoors in early spring; direct sow in late spring

Planting out: Around last frost

Spacing: 12"

Growing

Chinese Forget-me-not prefers **full sun** or **partial shade**. The soil should be of **average fertility, moist** and **well drained**. A heavy clay or overly fertile soil will cause floppy, unattractive growth.

C. amabile (this page)

Tips

The foliage of Chinese Forget-me-not is not exceptionally attractive, and it is best planted in masses or used to fill in the space under shrubs and other tall border plants.

This plant self-seeds quite readily and may return for many seasons. Be careful it doesn't overtake your garden. Removing the flowerheads right before they seed will keep this situation under control.

The genus name comes from the Greek kyon, *'dog,' and* glossum, *'tongue,' referring to the shape of the leaves.*

Recommended

C. amabile forms an upright plant that branches strongly. It bears bright blue or sometimes white or pink flowers in small clusters. **'Blue Showers'** grows about 24" tall and bears attractive, light blue flowers. **'Firmament'** ('Firmament Blue') is a compact variety, about 12–18" tall, with hairy gray leaves. The pendulous flowers are sky blue.

Problems & Pests

This plant is subject to root and stem rot and mildew, problems that can be avoided by not overwatering.

Cleome
Spider Flower
Cleome

Height: 1–5' **Spread:** 18–36" **Flower color:** pink, rose, violet, white

NATIVE TO SOUTH AMERICA, these exotic-looking flowers have risen to stardom in Michigan gardens. Cleomes are available in white, pink and lavender, but if allowed to re-seed, the second generation usually reverts to the dominant parent color of light purple. In bright sun and reasonably fertile soil, cleomes often rise to 4' or more in height and then gracefully arch over and sway in the wind. Their form is part of their charm, so no staking is needed. 'Sparkler Blush,' a new dwarf cultivar up to 3' tall, was an All-America winner for 2002.

Planting

Seeding: Indoors in late winter; direct sow in spring

Planting out: After last frost

Spacing: 18–30"

Growing

Cleomes prefer **full sun** but tolerate partial shade. **Any kind of soil** will do fine. Mix in plenty of **organic matter** to help the soil retain moisture. These plants are drought tolerant but look and perform better if watered regularly. Don't water excessively or they will become leggy. Chill seeds overnight before planting.

Pinch out the center of a cleome plant when transplanting, and it will branch out to produce up to a dozen blooms.

Deadhead to prolong the blooming period and to minimize these plants' prolific self-sowing. Self-sowed seedlings will start coming up almost as soon as the seeds hit the ground and can become invasive. Fortunately, the new plants are very distinctive and can be spotted poking up where they don't belong, making them easy to pull up while they are still young. Flowers of self-sowed seedlings will most likely revert to purple, the original species' color.

Tips

Cleome can be planted in groups at the back of a border. These plants are also effective in the center of an island bed; use lower-growing plants around the edges to hide the leafless lower stems of the cleome.

C. h. 'Royal Queen' series (below)

Be careful when handling these plants because they have nasty barbs along the stems.

Recommended

C. hassleriana is a tall, upright plant with strong, supple, thorny stems. It grows up to 5' tall. The foliage and flowers of this plant have a strong, but not unpleasant, scent. **'Helen Campbell'** has white flowers. **'Royal Queen'** series has flowers in all colors, available by individual color or as a mixture of all available colors. The varieties are named by their color; e.g., **'Cherry Queen,'** **'Rose Queen'** and **'Violet Queen.'** Plants in this series resist fading. **'Sparkler Blush'** is a dwarf cultivar that grows up to 3' tall. It bears pink flowers that fade to white.

C. serrulata (Rocky Mountain Bee Plant) is native to western North America. It is rarely available commercially, but the dwarf cultivar **'Solo'** can be grown from seed. It grows 12–18" tall and bears 2–3", pink and white blooms. This plant is thornless.

Problems & Pests

Aphids may be a problem.

The flowers can be cut for fresh arrangements, although the plants have an unusual odor that is noticeable up close. You can also try adding the seedpods to dried arrangements.

'Spider flower' is another name for Cleome, but 'hummingbird flower' might be more appropriate. These plants bloom through to fall, providing nectar for the tiny birds after many other flowers have finished blooming.

C. h. 'Helen Campbell' (above), *Cleome* with *Nicotiana, Pelargonium* and *Impatiens* (below)

Cockscomb
Celosia, Woolflower
Celosia

Height: 10–36" **Spread:** usually equal to height
Flower color: red, orange, gold, yellow, pink, purple

ALTHOUGH THE NAME COCKSCOMB REFLECTS THE RESEMBLANCE of the crested types to a rooster's crest, the distorted flowers look brain-like to me. But when dried and combined with other everlastings in floral wreaths and swags, the flowerheads add rich texture and color to the designs. The plumed varieties in bright pink, gold and red also make lovely additions to both dried and fresh floral arrangements. With their upright growth habit and vivid plumage, cockscombs often look awkward mixed with other flowers in display gardens, but they are effective bunched together in a container or flowerbed.

To dry the plumes, pick the flowers when they are at their peak and hang them upside down in a cool, shaded place.

Planting

Seeding: Indoors in late winter; direct sow in mid- to late spring

Planting out: Once soil has warmed

Spacing: Depends on variety

Growing

A sheltered spot in full sun is best. The soil should be fertile and well drained with plenty of organic matter worked in. Cockscombs like to be watered regularly.

It is preferable to start cockscombs directly in the garden. If you need to start them indoors, start the seeds in peat pots or pellets and plant them into the garden before they begin to flower. If left too long in pots, cockscombs will suffer stunted growth and won't be able to adapt to the garden. Keep seeds moist while they are germinating and do not cover them.

Use the expected spread of the variety to determine the appropriate spacing. It will usually be between 6" and 18".

Plumosa Group (this page)

Tips

Use cockscombs in borders and beds as well as in planters. The flowers make interesting additions to cut arrangements, either fresh or dried. A mass planting of Plume Celosia looks bright and cheerful in the garden. The popular crested varieties work well as accents and as cut flowers.

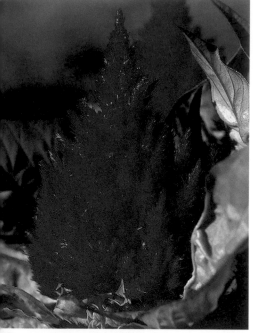

Plumosa Group (this page)

Recommended

C. argentea is the species from which both the crested and plume-type cultivars have been developed. The species itself is never grown. Cristata Group (Crested Celosia) has the blooms that resemble brains or rooster combs. This group has many varieties and cultivars. 'Jewel Box' bears flowers in red, pink, orange, yellow and gold on compact plants 10" tall. Plumosa Group (Plume Celosia) has feathery, plume-like blooms. This group also has many varieties and cultivars. 'Century' has neat, much-branched plants up to 24" tall and 18" in spread, with flowers in many bright colors. 'Fairy Fountains' is a compact plant, 12" tall, that bears long-lasting flowers

in red, yellow and pink. Another interesting recent development from the species is 'Startrek,' which has bright, pink-plumed flowers that radiate out from a central plume.

C. spicata '**Flamingo**' has spikes of pink or purple flowers that fade to white. It grows about 36" tall.

Problems & Pests

Cockscombs may develop root rot if planted out too early or if over-watered when first planted out. Cool, wet weather is the biggest problem.

The genus name Celosia *is derived from the Greek* keleos, *'burning,' referring to the intensely colorful blooms.*

C. a. 'Startrek' (above), Cristata Group (below)

Coleus

Solenostemon (Coleus)

Height: 6–36" or more **Spread:** usually equal to height
Flower color: light purple; plant grown for foliage

THE USE OF COLORFUL FOLIAGE IS A HOT TREND IN TODAY'S garden design, so Coleus, an old-time Victorian favorite, is all the rage in Michigan gardens. New hybrids that are vegetatively propagated grow larger, reaching 36" or more in height in a single season. These new kids on the block produce the most vibrant color when placed in full sun. Collectors who lack space to overwinter these beauties can take cuttings that quickly root in water or damp potting soil.

Planting

Seeding: Indoors in winter

Planting out: Once soil has warmed

Spacing: 12"

Growing

Seed-grown Coleus prefers to grow in **light or partial shade,** but it tolerates full shade if the shade isn't too dense and full sun if the plants are watered regularly. Cultivars propagated from cuttings thrive in **full sun** to **partial shade.** The soil for all Coleus should be of **rich to average fertility, humus rich, moist** and **well drained.**

Place the seeds in a refrigerator for one or two days before planting them on the soil surface. Cold temperatures will assist in breaking their dormancy. They need light to germinate. Seedlings will be green at first, but leaf variegation will develop as the plants mature.

Coleus is easy to propagate from stem cuttings, and in doing so you can ensure that you have a group of plants with the same leaf markings, shapes or colors. As your seedlings develop, decide which ones you like best, and when they are about three pairs of leaves high, pinch off the tip. The plants will begin to branch out.

Pinch all the tips off regularly as the branches grow to create a very

Although Coleus is a member of the mint family, with the characteristic square stems, it has none of the enjoyable culinary or aromatic qualities.

bushy plant from which you will be able to take a large number of cuttings. The cuttings should be about three leaf pairs long. Make the cut just below a leaf pair, and then remove the two bottom leaves. Plant the cuttings in pots filled with a soil mix intended for starting seeds. Keep the soil moist but not soggy. The plants should develop roots within a couple of weeks.

Tips

The bold, colorful foliage creates a dramatic display in beds and borders. Coleus can also be used in mixed containers and as an edging plant. It can be grown indoors as a houseplant in a bright room.

When flower buds develop, it is best to pinch them off, because the plants tend to stretch out and become less attractive after they flower.

Recommended

S. scutellarioides (Coleus blumei var. *verschaffeltii)* forms a bushy mound

of foliage. The leaf edges range from slightly toothed to very ruffled. The leaves are usually multi-colored with shades ranging from pale greenish yellow to deep purple-black. The size may be 6–36", depending on the cultivar, and the spread is usually equal to the height. Dozens of cultivars are available and many cannot be started from seed. A few interesting cultivars that can be started from seed are the **'Dragon'** series with bright yellow-green margins around variably colored leaves; **'Garnet Robe'** with a cascading habit and dark wine red leaves edged with yellow-green; **'Palisandra'** with velvety, purple-black foliage; **'Scarlet Poncho'** with wine red leaves edged with yellow-green; and the **'Wizard'** series with variegated foliage on compact plants.

Problems & Pests

Mealybugs, scale insects, aphids and whiteflies can cause occasional trouble.

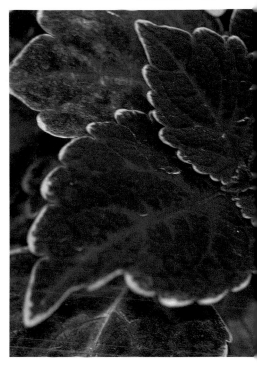

Coleus can be trained to grow into a standard (tree) form by pinching off the side branches as they grow. Once the plant reaches the desired height, pinch from the top.

Coreopsis
Coreopsis

Height: 8"–4' **Spread:** 8–18" **Flower color:** yellow, red, orange, brown

THESE NORTH AMERICAN NATIVES CAN BE FOUND IN THE ANNUAL border of Monet's garden at Giverny, France. Mainstays of many wildflower-garden mixes, coreopsis are drought tolerant and resent overfertilizing. After the first flush of blooms, they need deadheading to stay tidy, so if you are short on time plant them in a native setting where they can do their thing naturally. These plants readily re-seed but are unable to compete with weedy bullies that persist in meadows or naturalized plantings.

Planting

Seeding: Indoors in mid-winter; direct sow after last frost

Planting out: After last frost

Spacing: 8–12"

Growing

Coreopsis plants prefer **full sun**. The soil should be of **average to rich fertility, light** and **well drained**. Poor soil is also tolerated but with somewhat reduced flowering. Good drainage is the most important factor for these drought-tolerant plants.

Tips

Coreopsis plants look comfortable growing in front of a rustic wooden fence or repeating in clusters in a bed of perennials. They make a beautiful color combination planted with deep purple coral bells or royal purple heliotrope. Well suited to naturalized meadow plantings, coreopsis can also be used in informal beds and borders where they will flower all season if deadheaded regularly. These plants also produce lovely cut flowers.

Coreopsis plants can be blown over or have their stems broken during heavy rain or high winds. The fine foliage isn't dense enough to hide tomato or peony cages. Twiggy branches, inserted while the plants are small, will give the plants a support structure to grow up into. In very windy spots, it is best to use the dwarf forms of coreopsis.

Recommended

C. grandiflora forms a clump of stems and foliage. It grows 18–36" tall, spreads about 18" and bears bright yellow single flowers all summer. 'Early Sunrise' bears bright yellow double flowers on compact plants about 18" tall.

C. tinctoria (above), *C. g.* 'Early Sunrise' (below)

C. tinctoria forms a clump of basal leaves and tall, branching stems with just a few leaves. It grows up to 4' tall and spreads up to 18". The flowers are usually bright yellow with dark red bands at the petal bases; flowers in red, orange or brown are also possible. Dwarf cultivars that grow about 8–12" tall are available.

Problems & Pests

Slugs, snails and fungal diseases can be problems.

Self-seeding is likely with these plants, so they may pop up from year to year in the same area if left to their own devices.

Cosmos

Cosmos

Height: 1–7' **Spread:** 12–18" **Flower color:** magenta, pink, purple, white, yellow, gold, orange, red, scarlet, maroon

COSMOS ARE THE BACKBONE OF THE CLASSIC COTTAGE GARDEN, but for those who find the blowsy look of the old-fashioned 'Sensation' mix a little hard to handle, several other cultivars behave in a more restrained manner. 'Sonata' series offers dwarf plants that stay under 24". 'Sea Shells' features unusual tubular petals, and 'Psyche' bears semi-double flowers. In addition to the traditional colors of white, pink and maroon, cosmos also come in hot colors —bright gold, red and orange—that will spice up any landscape. Cosmos often re-seed throughout the garden, but pushy volunteers are easily removed.

The name Cosmos *is from the Greek and means 'beautiful.'*

Planting

Seeding: Indoors in late winter; direct sow after soil has warmed

Planting out: After last frost

Spacing: 12–18"

Growing

Cosmos like **full sun**. The soil should be of **poor or average fertility** and **well drained**. Cosmos are drought tolerant. Overfertilizing and overwatering can reduce the number of flowers produced. Yellow Cosmos will do better if sowed directly in the garden. Keep faded blooms cut to encourage more buds. Often, these plants re-seed themselves.

Although these plants may need staking, they are difficult to stake. Save yourself the trouble of staking by planting them in a sheltered location or against a fence. You could also grow shorter varieties. If staking can't be avoided, push twiggy branches into the ground when the plants are young and allow them to grow up between the branches to provide support. The branches will be hidden by the mature plants.

C. bipinnatus (this page)

Tips

Cosmos are attractive in cottage gardens, at the back of a border or mass planted in an informal bed or border.

Recommended

C. atrosanguineus (Chocolate Cosmos) has recently become popular among annual connoisseurs for its fragrant, deep maroon flowers that some claim smell like chocolate. The plant is upright, growing to 30" tall, but tends to flop over a bit when the stem gets too long.

C. bipinnatus (Annual Cosmos) has many cultivars. The flowers come in magenta, rose, pink or white, usually with yellow centers. Old varieties grow 3–6' tall, while some of the newer cultivars grow 12–36" tall. **'Daydream'** has white flowers flushed with pink at the petal bases. It grows up to 5' tall. **'Psyche'** bears large, showy, semi-double flowers in pink, white and red. **'Sea Shells'** has flowers in all colors and petals that are rolled into tubes. It grows up to 42" tall. **'Sensation'** bears large, white or pink flowers and grows up to 4' tall. **'Sonata'** series includes compact plants up to 24" tall that bear red, pink or white flowers.

C. sulphureus (Yellow Cosmos) has gold, orange, scarlet and yellow flowers. Old varieties grow 7' tall, and new varieties grow 1–4' tall. **'Klondike'** is a compact cultivar

C. bipinnatus (this page)

about 12–24" tall. Its single or semi-double flowers are bright yellow or orange-red. **'Ladybird'** series has compact dwarf plants, 12–14" tall, that rarely need staking. The foliage is not as feathered as it is in other cultivars.

Problems & Pests

Cosmos rarely have any problems, but watch for wilt, aster yellows, powdery mildew and aphids.

Cut flowers of cosmos make lovely, long-lasting fillers in arrangements.

C. atrosanguineus (above), *C. bipinnatus* (below)

Creeping Zinnia
Sanvitalia

Height: 4–8" **Spread:** 12–18" **Flower color:** yellow or orange with dark brown or purple centers

WHEN USED AS AN EDGER TO FRAME TALLER PLANTS IN CONTAINERS, Creeping Zinnia, with its trailing growth habit, will spill over the sides in such a relaxed, haphazard manner it might better be called Lazy Daisy. The showers of penny-sized, orange or yellow, daisy-like flowers with deep purple centers will slow when the hot weather arrives. When the temperatures come down again, the show will pick up.

Planting

Seeding: Direct sow in mid-spring

Planting out: After last frost

Spacing: 12"

Growing

Creeping Zinnia prefers **full sun.**
The soil should be of **average fertility,
light, sandy** and **well drained.**

Do not cover the seeds when you
sow them because they need light
to germinate.

Tips

Use Creeping Zinnia as an annual
groundcover or edging plant. It is
also dramatic in hanging baskets
and in mixed containers.

*The less you do for it, the better
this flowering plant will look.*

Creeping Zinnia is one of the easiest
annuals to grow. It is also one of the
easiest to damage with too much
care; overwatering and overfertilizing can quickly kill it.

Recommended

S. procumbens forms a low mat of
foliage up to 8" tall. Small yellow or
orange, daisy-like flowers with dark
centers are borne from summer
until long into fall. 'Sprite' is a
mounding plant that has yellow-
orange flowers with dark centers.
'Yellow Carpet' is a low-growing
dwarf variety that is up to 4" tall
and 18" wide. It has bright yellow
flowers with dark centers.

Problems & Pests

Keep Creeping Zinnia from getting
hit by a sprinkler system, or the
plant will suffer mildew and fungal
problems.

Cup Flower

Nierembergia

Height: 6–12" **Spread:** 6–12" **Flower color:** blue, purple or white, with yellow centers

LOVELY FOR PLANTING UNDER ROSES OR LANTANA STANDARDS, Cup Flower does best in moderately moist, humus-rich soil or potting soil that contains slow-release fertilizer. Deadheading is required to keep it blooming. Cup Flower belongs to the poisonous nightshade family, so be sure to keep it away from pets and small children.

Planting

Seeding: Indoors in mid-winter

Planting out: Spring

Spacing: 6–12"

Growing

Cup Flower grows well in **full sun** or **partial shade**. The soil should be of **average fertility, moist** and **well drained**. Fertilize little, if at all.

Cup Flower is a perennial used as an annual. During a mild winter, in the warmest parts of the state, it may survive the winter. Unfortunately, in these warm areas, it may suffer during the heat of summer. If your plant survives the winter, treat it as a bonus. It is often easier to start new plants each year than to try to protect mature plants.

'Mont Blanc' (this page)

Tips

Use Cup Flower as an annual ground-cover. It is also useful for edges of beds and borders, in rock gardens, on rock walls and in containers and hanging baskets. It grows best when summers are cool, and it can withstand a light frost.

Recommended

N. caerulea (N. hippomanica) forms a small mound of foliage. This plant bears delicate, cup-shaped flowers in lavender blue with yellow centers. **'Mont Blanc'** has white flowers with yellow centers. **'Purple Robe'** has deep purple flowers with golden eyes.

Problems & Pests

Slugs and snails are likely to be the worst problem for this plant. Because Cup Flower is susceptible to tobacco mosaic virus, don't plant it near any flowering tobacco or tomato plants.

The former species name hippomanica *is from the Greek and means 'drives horses crazy.' Whether they went crazy because they loved to eat it or from actually eating the plant is unclear.*

Dahlberg Daisy
Golden Fleece
Thymophylla

Height: 6–12" **Spread:** 12" **Flower color:** yellow, less commonly orange

THIS LOW-GROWING ANNUAL RELATIVE OF THE PERENNIAL fleabane reaches a height of only about 6", so with its daisy-shaped blooms and dainty, fern-like foliage, Dahlberg Daisy is best used as an edger in containers and hanging baskets. It may flag in the heat of summer, so place it in a spot where the pots will be protected from the hot afternoon sun.

Planting

Seeding: Indoors in mid-winter; direct sow in spring

Planting out: After last frost

Spacing: 8–12"

Growing

Plant Dahlberg Daisy in **full sun.** Any **well-drained** soil is suitable, although soil of **poor or average fertility** is preferred. Dahlberg Daisy prefers cool summers. In hot climates, it flowers in spring.

Direct-sowed plants may not flower until quite late in summer. For earlier blooms, start the seeds indoors. Don't cover the seeds, because they require light to germinate. Dahlberg Daisy may self-sow and reappear each year. Trimming your plants back when flowering seems to be slowing will encourage new growth and more blooms.

Tips

This attractive plant can be used along the edges of borders, along the tops of rock walls, or in hanging baskets or mixed containers. In any location where it can cascade over and trail down an edge, Dahlberg Daisy will look wonderful.

Recommended

T. tenuiloba (Dyssodia tenuiloba) forms a mound of ferny foliage. From spring until the summer heat causes it to fade, it produces many bright yellow, daisy-like flowers. Trim it back once the flowers fade, and it may revive in late summer as the weather cools.

Dahlberg Daisy has fragrant foliage that some people compare to a lemon-thyme scent; perhaps this is the origin of the name Thymophylla, *meaning 'thyme-leaf.'*

Dahlia

Dahlia

Height: 8"–5' **Spread:** 8–18" **Flower color:** purple, pink, white, yellow, orange, red, bicolored

IT'S UNFORTUNATE THAT THESE ONCE-POPULAR BEDDING flowers are not more widely grown today. Dahlias thrive on benign neglect and, once established, produce showstopping flowers nonstop from July through frost. They look great in the garden and also make lovely cut flowers. Gardeners who like to grow in-your-face flowers will love the huge, dinner-plate varieties. The smaller, seed-grown cultivars are attractive as edgings in beds and borders.

Planting

Seeding: Indoors in mid- to late winter; direct sow in spring

Planting out: After last frost

Spacing: 12"

Growing

Dahlias prefer **full sun**. The soil should be **fertile**, rich in **organic matter, moist** and **well drained**. Dahlias are tuberous perennials that are treated as annuals. Tubers can be purchased and started early indoors. The tubers can also be lifted in fall and stored over winter in slightly moist peat moss. Pot them and keep them in a bright room when they start sprouting in mid- to late winter.

If there is a particular size, color or form of dahlia that you want, it is best to start it from tubers of that type. Seed-grown dahlias show a great deal of variation in color and form because the seed is generally sold in mixed packages.

In order to keep dahlias blooming and attractive, it is essential to remove the spent blooms.

Tips

Dahlias make attractive, colorful additions to a mixed border. The smaller varieties make good edging plants and the larger ones make good replacement plants for shrubs. Varieties with unusual or interesting flowers are attractive specimen plants.

There are many dahlia cultivars, but breeders have yet to develop true blue, scented and frost-hardy varieties.

Semi-cactus type (above)

Informal decorative type (above), peony type (below)

Recommended

Of the many dahlia hybrids, most must be grown from tubers but a few can be started from seed with good results. Examples of seed-started dahlias include *D.* **'Figaro,'** which forms a round, compact plant 12–16" tall. The flowers are small, double or semi-double, come in a wide variety of colors, and grow and flower quickly. This plant looks very good grouped in a border or in containers. *D.* **'Harlequin'** forms compact plants that flower quickly from seed. Flowers are solid or bicolored, single or semi-double in many shades. Many hybrid seeds are sold in mixed packets based on flower shape, for example, collarette, decorative or peony flowered. Tubers of specific types and colors can be purchased in late winter and early spring.

Problems & Pests

There are a few problems a dahlia grower may encounter; aphids, powdery mildew and slugs are the most likely. If a worse problem afflicts your dahlias, it may be best to destroy the infected plants and start over.

Dahlia flowers are categorized by size, from giants with blooms more than 10" in diameter to mignons with blooms up to 2" in diameter. They are also categorized by flower type—for example, peony, formal and informal decorative, semi-cactus and waterlily.

In the 18th century, the first European breeders of these Mexican plants were more interested in them as a possible food source. The blooms were thought to be unexceptional.

Diascia

Diascia

Twinspur

Diascia

Height: 8–12" **Spread:** 20" **Flower color:** shades of pink

ALTHOUGH RELATIVELY NEW ON THE
gardening scene, diascias are quickly
becoming a favorite with Michigan gardeners. These low growers are excellent
choices for the front of border plantings
and work equally well as fillers for containers. The alternative common name
twinspur comes from the two tiny spikes
that jut out from the back of each blossom.
Some say the blossoms resemble snapdragons, but to my eye they
look more like miniature
orchids. Salmon pink is
the most common
flower color, but
diascias' color range
stretches from white
to pink to a pretty,
pale red.

Planting

Seeding: Indoors in spring

Planting out: After the last frost

Spacing: 18"

Growing

Diascias prefer **full sun** but enjoy protection from the afternoon sun when the weather is hot and humid. The soil should be **fertile, moist** and **well drained.** Diascias are generally frost hardy and bloom well into fall.

These plants don't thrive in high humidity and heat. Plants may fade during the hottest part of summer but will revive and produce flowers as temperatures drop in fall. Diascias are perennials treated as an annuals in most of North America.

Deadheading will keep the blooms coming, and if flowering becomes sparse in searing summer heat, shearing will encourage a fresh flush of blooms in a few weeks when the weather cools.

Tips

Diascias are attractive in a rock garden or mass planted in a border. Pinch tips of plants to increase bushiness.

'Strawberry Sundae'

D. barberae cultivar

Recommended

D. barberae is a low-growing plant that bears loose spikes of pink flowers from mid-summer to frost. **'Blackthorn Apricot'** has apricot-colored flowers and flowerheads that point downwards. **'Pink Queen'** has light, shimmery pink flowers on long, slender stalks.

D. **'Coral Belle'** is a quick-growing hybrid that forms a dense mound of bright green foliage. The flowers are a delicate coral pink.

D. **'Strawberry Sundae'** is a fairly compact plant with trailing stems and bright pink flowers.

Problems & Pests

Watch out for snails and slugs.

Dusty Miller
Senecio

Height: 12–24" **Spread:** equal to height or slightly narrower
Flower color: yellow or white; plant grown for silvery foliage

WITH ITS ELEGANT, SOFT, SILVER LEAVES, DUSTY MILLER MAKES
a charming companion plant that contrasts nicely with vibrant pink and purple
petunias and other brightly colored annuals in both beds and containers. Pair
it with light pinks, gentle mauves and other pastels for a look of quiet elegance.
When cut for fresh or dried floral arrangements, Dusty Miller makes a wonderful filler that adds a lacy texture.

Planting

Seeding: Indoors in mid-winter

Planting out: Spring

Spacing: 12"

Growing

Dusty Miller prefers **full sun** but tolerates light shade. The soil should be of **average fertility** and **well drained**.

Tips

The soft, silvery, lacy leaves of this plant are its main feature, and it is used primarily as an edging plant. It is also used in beds, borders and containers. The silvery foliage makes a good backdrop to show off the brightly colored flowers of other plants.

Pinch off the flowers before they bloom. They aren't showy and steal energy that would otherwise go to the foliage.

Recommended

S. cineraria forms a mound of fuzzy, silvery gray, lobed or finely divided foliage. Many cultivars have been developed with impressive foliage colors and shapes. 'Cirrus' has lobed, silvery green or white foliage. 'Silver Dust' has deeply lobed, silvery white foliage. 'Silver Lace' has delicate, silvery white foliage that glows in the moonlight.

Mix Dusty Miller with geraniums, begonias, marigolds or cockscombs to really bring out the vibrant colors of these flowers.

Dwarf Morning Glory
Convolvulus

Height: 6–16" **Spread:** 10–12" **Flower color:** blue, purple, pink

IF YOU LOVE MORNING GLORIES BUT LACK THE SPACE TO GROW them, try this little cutie as a border edger and in containers and window boxes. One of the most popular cultivars, 'Royal Ensign,' sports royal blue petals with white throats and yellow centers. Excellent drainage is a big key to success so use a good soil-less potting mix when planting Dwarf Morning Glory in pots.

Planting

Seeding: Indoors in late winter; direct sow in mid- or late spring

Planting out: Mid- or late spring

Spacing: 8–12"

Growing

Dwarf Morning Glory prefers **full sun.** The soil should be of **poor or average fertility** and **well drained.** This plant may not flower well in rich, moist soil.

Soak the seeds in water overnight before planting them. If starting seeds early indoors, plant them in peat pots to avoid root damage when transplanting.

Tips

Dwarf Morning Glory is a compact, mounding plant that can be grown on rock walls or in borders, containers or hanging baskets.

This easy-care plant is rarely plagued by pests or diseases.

Recommended

C. tricolor bears flowers that last only a single day, blooming in the morning and twisting shut that evening. The species grows 12–16" tall. **'Ensign'** series has low-growing, spreading plants growing 6" tall. **'Royal Ensign'** has deep blue flowers with white and yellow throats. **'Star of Yalta'** bears deep purple flowers that pale to violet in the throat.

This annual is related to the dreaded bindweeds (Convolvulus arvensis *and* C. sepium)*, but it doesn't share the unstoppable twining and spreading power of its weedy cousins.*

Fan Flower

Scaevola

Height: up to 8" **Spread:** up to 36" or more **Flower color:** blue, purple

FAN FLOWER IS ONE OF THE NEWER KIDS ON THE BLOCK, BUT IT is fast becoming a darling of the container crowd. Its popularity is well deserved. Give this Australian import sunny conditions, well-drained soil, and an occasional pinch or two and it will flower exuberantly from April through to frost. Plant Fan Flower around the edge of a container of white Zonal Geranium for a showy, high-contrast display.

Planting

Seeding: Indoors in late winter

Planting out: After last frost

Spacing: 2–4'

Regular pinching and trimming will keep your Fan Flower bushy and blooming.

Growing

Fan Flower grows well in **full sun** or **light shade**. The soil should be of **average fertility, moist** and **well drained**. Water regularly, because this plant doesn't like to dry out completely. It does, however, recover quickly from wilting when watered.

This attractive plant is actually a perennial that is treated as an annual. Cuttings can be taken during summer and new plants grown indoors to be used the following summer, or a plant can be brought in and kept in a bright room over winter. Seeds can be difficult to find.

Tips

Fan Flower is popular for hanging baskets and containers, but it can also be used along the tops of rock walls and in rock gardens where it can trail down. This plant makes an interesting addition to mixed borders or can be used under shrubs, where the long, trailing stems of Fan Flower will form an attractive groundcover.

Recommended

S. aemula forms a mound of foliage from which trailing stems emerge. The fan-shaped flowers come in shades of purple, usually with white bases. The species is rarely grown because there are many improved cultivars. **'Blue Wonder,'** a Proven Winners cultivar, has long, trailing branches, making it ideal for hanging baskets. It can eventually spread 36" or more. **'Saphira'** is a new compact variety with deep blue flowers. It spreads about 12".

Problems & Pests

Whiteflies may cause problems for Fan Flower if the plant becomes stressed from lack of water.

Flowering Flax

Linum

Height: 18–30" **Spread:** 6" **Flower color:** pink, white, red, blue, purple

GARDENERS WHO ARE NOT FAMILIAR with this colorful character usually fall in love with it at first sight. As soon as the ground can be worked, sow the seed where the plants are to flower. The bright red or baby blue flowers will begin to put on a lovely show in spring and will continue nonstop as long as the weather stays cool. They make for a colorful debut of a mixed perennial border and set the stage for the next act.

Planting

Seeding: Direct sow in mid-spring

Planting out: Around last frost

Spacing: 4–6"

Growing

Flowering Flax grows well in **full sun,** but during the heat of summer it enjoys protection from the hot afternoon sun. The soil should be of **average fertility, light, humus rich** and **well drained.**

Tips

Flowering Flax can be used in borders and mixed containers and will nicely fill in the spaces between young perennials and shrubs in the landscape.

Recommended

L. grandiflorum is an upright, branching plant. It grows 18–30" tall and spreads about 6". It bears dark-centered, light pink flowers. '**Bright Eyes**' bears white flowers with dark red or brown centers. It grows about 18" tall. '**Caeruleum**' bears blue or purple flowers. '**Rubrum**' bears deep red flowers on plants that grow 18" tall.

Problems & Pests

Excess moisture can cause trouble with stem rot and damping off. Slugs, snails and aphids can also cause problems.

The related L. usitatissimum *is the source of linen fiber and the flax seeds used to produce oil. It has been in cultivation for more than 7000 years.*

Four-O'Clock Flower

Mirabilis

Height: 18–36" **Spread:** 18–24" **Flower color:** red, pink, magenta, yellow, white or bicolored

EVERYTHING OLD IS NEW AGAIN, AND THAT'S CERTAINLY TRUE when it comes to Four-o'clock Flower, which has come in and out of fashion. It is now in again. As the name suggests, the flowers open late in the afternoon. They persist until sunrise, though, so if you entertain in the evening, plant a stand of this beauty next to your patio or deck. It will reward you with a lovely soft fragrance as well as a colorful show.

Planting

Seeding: Indoors in late winter; direct sow in mid-spring

Planting out: Mid-spring

Spacing: 16–24"

Growing

Four-o'clock Flower prefers **full sun** but tolerates partial shade. The soil should be **fertile,** though any **well-drained** soil is tolerated.

This plant is a perennial that is treated as an annual, and it may be grown from tuberous roots. Dig up the roots in fall and re-plant in spring to enjoy larger plants.

Tips

Four-o'clock Flower can be used in beds, borders, containers and window boxes. The flowers are scented, so the plant is often located near deck patios or terraces where the scent can be enjoyed in the afternoon and evening.

Recommended

M. jalapa forms a bushy mound of foliage. The flowers may be solid or bicolored. A single plant may bear flowers of several colors.

Problems & Pests

This plant has very few problems as long as it is given well-drained soil.

Many species of moths are attracted to the flowers of this plant, which may bloom in several colors on a single plant.

Fuchsia

Fuchsia

Height: 6–36" **Spread:** 6–36" **Flower color:** pink, orange, red, purple or white; often bicolored

A HANGING BASKET OF FUCHSIA IN BLOOM demands to be the center of attention. The upright varieties that sport single blooms may not be as showy as the flashy trailers, but some uprights, such as 'Gartenmeister Bonstedt,' with its bronze-tinged foliage and bright orange flowers, make a nice accent mixed with burgundy-leaved Coleus and other light-shade lovers. Take care to keep fuchsias well watered and out of the heat and direct sun in high summer or they will quickly crash and burn.

Children, and some adults, enjoy popping the fat buds of fuchsias. The temptation to squeeze them is almost irresistible.

Planting

Seeding: Not recommended

Planting out: After last frost

Spacing: 12–24"

Growing

Fuchsias are grown in **partial or light shade.** They are generally not tolerant of summer heat, and full sun can be too hot for them. The soil should be **fertile, moist** and **well drained.**

Fuchsias need to be well watered, particularly in hot weather. Ensure that the soil has good drainage because otherwise the plants can develop rot problems. Fuchsias planted in well-aerated soil with plenty of perlite are almost impossible to overwater. As summer wears on, increase the amount of water given to container plants as the pots and baskets fill with thirsty roots. Fuchsias bloom on new growth, which will be stimulated by a high-nitrogen plant food.

Some fuchsias can be started from seed, although the germination rate can be poor and erratic. If you are up for the challenge, start the plants indoors in mid-winter. Ensure that the soil is warm, at 68°–75° F. Seeds can take from two weeks to two months to sprout. Plants will start to flower only when the days have more than 13 hours of light. It may be late summer before you see any reward for your efforts.

Although fuchsias are hard to start from seed, they are easy to propagate from cuttings. Snip off 6" of new tip growth, remove the leaves

'Winston Churchill' (above)

from the lower third of the stem and insert the cuttings into soft soil or perlite. Once rooted and potted, the plants will bloom all summer.

Tips

The upright fuchsias can be used in mixed planters, beds and borders. The pendulous fuchsias are most often used in hanging baskets, but these flowers dangling from flexible branches also make attractive additions to planters and rock gardens.

Fuchsias should be deadheaded. Pluck the swollen seedpods from behind the fading petals or the seeds will ripen and rob the plant of energy necessary for flower production.

Fuchsias are perennials that are grown as annuals. To store fuchsias over winter, cut back the plants to 6" stumps after the first light frost and place them in a dark, cold, but not freezing, location. Water just enough to keep the soil barely moist and do not feed. In mid-spring, re-pot the stumps, set them near a bright window and fertilize them lightly. Set your overwintered

'Snowburner' (center)

plants outdoors the following spring after all danger of frost has passed.

Recommended

F. x *hybrida.* There are dozens of cultivars; just a few examples are given here. The upright fuchsias grow 18–36" tall, and the pendulous fuchsias grow 6–24" tall. Many of the available hybrids cannot be started from seed. 'Deep Purple' has purple petals and white sepals. 'Gartenmeister Bonstedt' is an upright, shrubby cultivar that grows about 24" tall and bears tubular, orange-red flowers. The foliage is bronzy red with purple undersides. 'Snowburner' has white petals and pink sepals. 'Swingtime' has white petals with pink bases and pink sepals. This plant grows 12–24" tall and spreads about 6". It can be grown in a hanging basket or as a relaxed upright plant in beds and borders. 'Winston Churchill' has purple petals and pink sepals. The plant grows 8–30" tall, with an equal spread. It is quite upright in form but is often grown in hanging baskets.

Problems & Pests

Aphids, spider mites and whiteflies are common insect pests. Diseases such as crown rot, root rot and rust can be avoided with good air circu lation and drainage.

Some gardeners who have kept fuchsias over several years have trained their plants to adopt a tree form.

Gazania

Gazania

Height: usually 6–8"; may reach 12–18" **Spread:** 8–12"
Flower color: red, orange, yellow, pink, cream

DROUGHT- AND HEAT-TOLERANT GAZANIA IS THE PERFECT PLANT for edging cement walkways and driveways that bake all day in the heat of the sun. The 3–4" wide, daisy-like flowers come in bright, eye-catching shades of yellow, orange and pink. They make colorful additions to herb gardens and rockeries where there is good drainage and little chance of overwatering. Mix Gazania with other drought-tolerant plants and you can create a colorful carpet in a xeriscape garden.

Planting

Seeding: Indoors in late winter; direct sow after last frost

Planting out: After last frost

Spacing: 6–10"

Growing

Gazania grows best in **full sun** but tolerates some shade. The soil should be of **poor to average fertility, sandy** and **well drained**. This plant grows best in hot weather over 80° F.

Tips

Low-growing Gazania makes an excellent groundcover and is also useful on exposed slopes, in mixed containers and as an edging in flowerbeds.

Recommended

G. rigens forms a low basal rosette of lobed foliage. Large, daisy-like flowers with pointed petals are borne on strong stems above the plant. The petals often have a contrasting stripe or spot. The flowers tend to close on gloomy days and in low-light situations. The species is rarely grown, but several hybrid cultivars are available. **'Daybreak'** series bears flowers in many colors, often with a contrasting stripe down the center of each petal. These flowers will stay open on dull days but close on rainy or very dark days. **'Kiss'** series bears large flowers in several colors on compact plants. Seeds are available by individual flower color or as a mix. **'Mini-Star'** series has compact plants and flowers in many colors with a contrasting dot at the base of each petal. **'Sundance'** bears flowers in reds and yellows with dark, contrasting stripes down the centers of the petals.

Problems & Pests

Overwatering is the likely cause of any problems for this plant.

'Sundance' (above), mixed hybrids (below)

This native of southern Africa has very few pests and transplants easily, even when in bloom.

Geranium

Pelargonium

Height: 8–36" **Spread:** 6"–4' **Flower color:** red, pink, violet, orange, salmon, white, purple

IF YOU THINK GERANIUMS ARE BORING, YOU'VE BEEN HANGING around with the wrong crowd. Newer varieties sporting colorful foliage and interesting flowers with showstopping color have given these easy-to-grow plants a fresh and exciting look. The cascading Ivy-leaved Geranium, with shiny, bright green leaves and clusters of colorful double and semi-double blossoms, makes an easy-care addition to hanging baskets and containers. The columnar geraniums such as 'Pillar Salmon,' planted four to a pot and staked, look like miniature flowering trees. For added interest skirt them with a shower of Fan Flower.

Planting

Seeding: Indoors in early winter

Planting out: After last frost

Spacing: Zonal Geranium, about 12"; Ivy-leaved Geranium, 24–36"

Growing

Geraniums prefer **full sun** but tolerate partial shade, although they may not bloom as profusely. The soil should be **fertile** and **well drained**.

P. zonale (above), *P. peltatum* with *Helichrysum* and *Solenostemon* (below)

Geraniums are slow to grow from seed, so purchasing plants may prove easier. However, if you would like to try starting your own from seed, start them indoors in early winter and cover them with clear plastic to maintain humidity until they germinate. Once the seedlings have three or four leaves, transplant them into individual 3–4" pots. Keep them in bright locations because they need lots of light to maintain their compact shape.

Deadheading is essential to keep geraniums blooming and looking neat. The flowerheads are attached to long stems that break off easily where they attach to the plant. Some gardeners prefer to snip off just the flowering end in order to avoid potentially damaging the stem.

Tips

Geraniums are very popular annual plants. Use Zonal Geranium in beds, borders and containers. Ivy-leaved Geranium is most often used in hanging baskets and containers to take advantage of its trailing habit, but it is also interesting used as a bedding plant to form a bushy, spreading groundcover.

Geraniums are perennials that are treated as annuals. They can be kept indoors over winter in a bright room.

P. zonale cultivar (above), P. peltatum (below)

Recommended

The following species and varieties are some of the easier ones to start from seed. Many popular varieties can be propagated only from cuttings and must be purchased as plants.

P. peltatum (Ivy-leaved Geranium) grows up to 12" tall and up to 4' wide. Many colors are available. Plants in the '**Summer Showers**' series can take four or more months to flower from seed. The '**Tornado**' series is very good for hanging baskets and containers. The plants are quite compact, and the flowers are either lilac or white.

P. zonale (Zonal Geranium) grows up to 24" tall and 12" wide. Dwarf varieties grow up to 8" tall and 6" wide. The flowers are red, pink, purple, orange or white. '**Orbit**' series has attractive, early-blooming, compact plants. The seed is often sold in a mixed packet, but some individual colors are available. '**Pillar**' series includes upright plants that grow up to 36" tall with staking. Salmon, violet and orange flowers are available.

'Pinto' series is available in all colors, and seed is generally sold by the color so you don't have to purchase a mixed packet and hope you like the colors you get.

Problems & Pests

Aphids will flock to overfertilized plants, but they can usually be washed off before they do much damage. Leaf spot and blight may bother geraniums growing in cool, moist soil.

Edema is an unusual condition to which geraniums are susceptible. This disease occurs when a plant is overwatered and the leaf cells burst. A warty surface develops on the leaves. There is no cure, although it can be avoided by watering carefully and removing any damaged leaves as the plant grows. The condition is more common in Ivy-leaved Geranium.

P. zonale cultivar (above), *P. peltatum* & *P. zonale* with *Rudbeckia* cultivar (below)

Ivy-leaved Geranium is one of the most beautiful plants to include in a mixed hanging basket or container.

Globe Amaranth

Gomphrena

Height: 6–30" **Spread:** 6–15" **Flower color:** purple, orange, magenta, pink, white, sometimes red

THE CLOVER-LIKE HEADS WE TEND TO REGARD AS THE FLOWERS of Globe Amaranth are actually brightly colored bracts (modified leaves) from which the miniscule flowers emerge. This plant was once cultivated in fields for use in fresh and dried floral arrangements. It has become popular for flowerbeds and container gardens with the introduction of tidy, compact varieties such as the brilliant orange-red 'Strawberry Fields.'

Globe Amaranth flowers are popular for cutting and drying because they keep their color and form well when dried. Harvest the blooms when they become round and plump, before the tiny flowers emerge, and dry them upside down in a cool, dry location.

Planting

Seeding: Indoors in late winter

Planting out: After last frost

Spacing: 10"

Growing

Globe Amaranth prefers **full sun.** The soil should be of **average fertility** and **well drained.** This plant likes hot weather. It needs watering only when drought-like conditions persist.

Seeds will germinate more quickly if soaked in water for two to four days before sowing. They need warm soil above 70° F to sprout.

The long-lasting flowers require only occasional deadheading.

G. globosa (this page), with nasturtiums (below)

Problems & Pests

Globe Amaranth is susceptible to some fungal diseases, such as gray mold and leaf spot.

Tips

Use Globe Amaranth in an informal or cottage garden. This plant is often underused because it doesn't start flowering until later in summer than many other annuals. Don't overlook it—the blooms are worth the wait and provide color from mid-summer until the first frost.

Recommended

G. globosa forms a rounded, bushy plant 12–24" tall that is dotted with papery, clover-like flowers in purple, magenta, white or pink. '**Buddy**' has more compact plants, 6–12" tall, with deep purple flowers. '**Lavender Lady**' grows into a large plant, up to 24" tall, and bears lavender purple flowers.

G. '**Strawberry Fields**' is a hybrid with bright orange-red or red flowers. It grows about 30" tall and spreads about half as much.

Godetia
Clarkia, Satin Flower
Clarkia (Godetia)

Height: 8–36" **Spread:** 10–12" **Flower color:** pink, red, purple, white, some bicolored

THESE GORGEOUS FLOWERING PLANTS MAY BE DIFFICULT TO FIND as transplants because they are cool-weather characters that quickly fade when hot, humid weather approaches. Often called by the name satin flower, godetias are valued by the floral industry for their cut flowers and fresh stems. If they are cut when the buds have swelled and are just beginning to open, they will last as long as two weeks in a vase.

Planting

Seeding: Direct sow in spring for summer bloom or in mid- to late summer for fall bloom

Spacing: 6"

Growing

Godetias will grow equally well in **full sun** or **light shade**. The soil should be **well drained, light, sandy** and of **poor or average fertility**. These plants don't like to be overwatered, so water sparingly and be sure to let them dry out between waterings. They do best in cool weather.

Starting seeds indoors is not recommended. Seed plants where you want them to grow because they are difficult to transplant. Thin seedlings to about 6" apart.

Tips

Godetias are useful in beds, borders, containers and rock gardens. The flowers can be used in fresh arrangements.

Recommended

C. amoena (Godetia amoena, G. grandiflora) (Godetia, Satin Flower) is a bushy, upright plant. It grows up to 30" tall, spreads 12" and bears clusters of ruffled, cup-shaped flowers in shades of pink, red, white and purple. **'Satin'** series has compact plants that grow 8–12" tall. The single flowers come in many colors, including some bicolors.

C. unguiculata (C. elegans) (Clarkia, Rocky Mountain Garland Flower) is a tall, branching plant that grows 12–36" tall and spreads up to 10". Its small, ruffled flowers can be pink, purple, red or white. **'Apple Blossom'** bears apricot pink double flowers. **'Royal Bouquet'** bears very ruffled double flowers in pink, red or light purple.

C. amoena (this page)

Problems & Pests

Root rot can occur in poorly drained soil.

These plants produce gorgeous, showy flowers despite their preference for poor soil.

Heliotrope
Cherry Pie Plant
Heliotropium

Height: 8"–4' **Spread:** 12–24" **Flower color:** purple, blue, white

BEAUTIFUL BUNDLES OF TINY, VIOLET BLUE OR WHITE FLOWERS with an intense vanilla-like fragrance, together with dark, elegantly textured foliage, make this shrubby annual a treasure in the garden. I use it to color up my herb garden, partnering it with variegated and purple sages and miniature pink roses. It requires little maintenance, and the flowers persist for weeks. A small 6–8" transplant will quickly develop into a 24" shrub, making it a good choice to fill in around roses.

Planting

Seeding: Indoors in mid-winter

Planting out: Once soil has warmed

Spacing: 12–18"

Growing

Heliotrope grows best in **full sun.**
The soil should be **fertile,** rich in
organic matter, moist and **well
drained.** Although overwatering
will kill Heliotrope, if left to dry
to the point of wilting, the plant
will be slow to recover.

Heliotrope is sensitive to cold
weather, so plant it out after all
danger of frost has passed. Protect
plants with newspaper or a floating
row cover (available at garden centers) if an unexpected late frost or
cold snap should arrive. Container-
grown plants can be brought
indoors at night if frost is expected.

Tips

Heliotrope is ideal for growing in
containers or beds near windows
and patios where the wonderful
scent of the flowers can be enjoyed.

This plant can be pinched and
shaped into a tree form, or standard, by pinching off the lower
branches as the plant grows until it
reaches the desired height and then
pinching the top to encourage the
plant to bush out. Create a shorter,
bushy form by pinching all the tips
that develop.

Heliotrope can be grown indoors
as a houseplant in a sunny window.
A plant may survive for years if kept
outdoors all summer and indoors
all winter in a cool, bright room.

H. arborescens (all pictures)

Recommended

H. arborescens is a low, bushy shrub that is treated as an annual. It grows 18–24" tall, with an equal spread. Large clusters of purple, blue or white, scented flowers are produced all summer. Some new cultivars are not as strongly scented as the species. **'Blue Wonder,'** however, is a compact plant that was developed for heavily scented flowers. Plants grow up to 16" tall with dark purple flowers. **'Dwarf Marine'** ('Mini Marine') is a compact, bushy plant with fragrant, purple flowers. It grows 8–12" tall and also makes a good houseplant for a bright location. **'Fragrant Delight'** is an older cultivar with royal purple flowers of intense fragrance. It can reach a height of 4' if grown as a standard. **'Marine'** has violet blue flowers and grows about 18" tall.

Problems & Pests

Aphids and whiteflies can be problems.

This old-fashioned flower may have been popular in your grandmother's day. Its recent return to popularity comes as no surprise considering its attractive foliage, flowers and scent.

Hollyhock

Alcea

Height: 5–8' **Spread:** 24" **Flower color:** yellow, white, apricot, pink, red, purple, reddish black

HOLLYHOCKS HAVE BEEN GRACING OUR gardens since colonial times. When I was a child, hollyhocks were often planted in alleyways in the heart of the city to create a beautiful living screen. Needing little more than sun and water, these prolific re-seeders can still be found gracing long-abandoned lots. Plant them along a section of white picket fence or sunny, south-facing wall to claim your own piece of history. For an interesting combination, plant morning glories among your hollyhocks and let them climb up the tall stalks.

Hollyhocks were originally grown as food plants. The leaves were added to salads.

Planting

Seeding: Start indoors in mid-winter

Planting out: After last frost

Spacing: 18–24"

Growing

Hollyhocks prefer **full sun** but tolerate partial shade. The soil should be **average to rich** and **well drained**.

Plant hollyhocks in a different part of the garden each year to keep hollyhock rust at bay.

Tips

Because they are so tall, hollyhocks look best at the back of the border or in the center of an island bed. In a windy location they will need to be staked. Plant them against a fence or wall for support.

If the main stem is pinched out early in the season, hollyhocks will be shorter and bushier with smaller flower spikes. These shorter stems are less likely to be broken by wind and can be left unstaked.

Old-fashioned types typically have single flowers, and they grow much taller and are more disease resistant than newer hybrids.

Recommended

A. rosea forms a rosette of basal leaves; the tall stalk that develops bears ruffled single or double blooms. **'Chater's Double'** bears double flowers in a wide range of colors. **'Nigra'** bears reddish black single flowers with yellow centers. **'Summer Carnival'** bears double flowers in yellows and reds.

A. rosea

It blooms in early summer and produces flowers lower on the stem than the other cultivars.

A. rugosa (Russian Hollyhock) is similar to *A. rosea* but is more resistant to hollyhock rust. It bears pale yellow to orangy yellow single flowers.

Problems & Pests

Hollyhock rust is the biggest problem. Hollyhocks are also susceptible to bacterial and fungal leaf spot. Slugs and cutworms occasionally attack young growth. Sometimes mallow flea beetles, aphids or Japanese beetles cause trouble.

'Nigra' (above), *A. rosea* (below)

*The powdered roots of plants
in the mallow family, to which
hollyhocks belong, were once
used to make soft lozenges to
soothe sore throats. Though
popular around the campfire,
marshmallows no longer contain
the throat-soothing properties
they originally did.*

A. *rosea* (below), 'Chater's Double' (right)

Hyacinth Bean
Egyptian Bean, Lablab Bean
Lablab (Dolichos)

Height: 10–15' **Spread:** variable **Flower color:** purple, white; also grown for purple pods

COLORFUL CLIMBERS ARE HOT COMMODITIES IN THE GARDEN THESE days, and Hyacinth Bean is in the running for top honors. Prized for its large, spiked flower clusters of decorative purple beans, this plant also has a place in American history. It appealed to Thomas Jefferson, who built a special arbor so he could grow and enjoy it in the garden at Monticello. More recently, Hyacinth Bean played a starring role in a fabulous display at the 4-H Children's Garden on the Michigan State University campus, securing it a place in Michigan gardens.

The purple pods are edible if thoroughly cooked with two to four changes of water. Try adding the cooked beans to a stir-fry to add some unusual color.

Planting

Seeding: Direct sow around last frost date, or start indoors in peat pots in early spring

Planting out: After last frost

Spacing: 12–18"

Growing

Hyacinth Bean prefers **full sun**. The soil should be **average to fertile, moist** and **well drained**. Feed this plant weekly to encourage plentiful flowering.

Tips

Hyacinth Bean needs a trellis, net, pole or other structure to twine up. Plant it against a fence or near a balcony.

The raw beans contain a cyanide-releasing chemical. Boiling and changing the water several times removes the chemical.

Recommended

L. purpureus (*Dolichos lablab*) is a vigorous twining vine. It can grow up to 30' tall, but when grown as an annual it grows about 10–15' tall. It bears many purple or white flowers over the summer, followed by deep purple pods.

Problems & Pests

Rare problems with leaf spot can occur.

Impatiens

Impatiens

Height: 6–36" **Spread:** 12–24" **Flower color:** shades of purple, red, burgundy, pink, yellow, orange, apricot, white; also bicolored

THE ENGLISH NAMED ONE OF THESE CAREFREE BLOOMERS BUSY Lizzie because it flowers nonstop through the growing season. Their exuberant flowering also explains why impatiens are America's top-selling bedding plants. To add punch to a partial-shade planting, mix lilac impatiens with purple nicotianas. A container of pink impatiens accented with the purple and silver foliage of Persian Shield makes for a spectacular combination. New Guinea Impatiens, originally introduced at Longwood Gardens in 1970, made a meteoric rise to popularity in the late '90s, thanks to careful breeding that produced larger flowers framed with fabulous foliage.

Impatiens come in a wide variety of heights, so be sure to check the tags before buying.

Planting

Seeding: Indoors in mid-winter; Balsam Impatiens indoors in late winter

Planting out: Once soil has warmed

Spacing: 12–18"

Growing

All impatiens do best in **partial shade** but tolerate full shade or, if kept moist, full sun. Of the various impatiens, New Guinea Impatiens and Balsam Impatiens are the best adapted to sunny locations. The soil should be **fertile, humus rich, moist** and **well drained**. New Guinea Impatiens does not like wet feet, so good drainage is a must.

Don't cover the seeds—they germinate best when exposed to light.

Tips

Busy Lizzie is known for its ability to grow and flower profusely in even deep shade. Mass plant in beds under trees, along shady fences or walls or in porch planters. It also looks lovely in hanging baskets. The new double-flowering varieties, such as 'Fiesta,' work beautifully as accent plants in hosta and wildflower gardens.

New Guinea Impatiens is almost shrubby in form and is popular in patio planters, beds and borders. It grows well in full sun and may not flower as profusely in deep shade. This plant is grown as much for its variegated leaves as for its flowers.

Balsam Impatiens was a popular garden plant in the Victorian era and has recently experienced a comeback in popularity. The habit

The name Impatiens refers to the impatient nature of the seedpods. When ripe, the seedpods burst open at the slightest touch and scatter their seeds.

I. hawkeri

of this plant is more upright than that of the other two impatiens, and it is attractive when grouped in beds and borders.

Recommended

New impatiens varieties are introduced every year, expanding the selection of size, form and color. The following list includes varieties that are popular year after year.

I. balsamina (Balsam Impatiens) grows 12–36" tall and up to 18" wide. The flowers come in shades of purple, red, pink or white. There are several double-flowered cultivars, such as **'Camellia-flowered,'** with pink, red or white flowers on plants up to 24" tall; **'Tom Thumb,'** with pink, red, purple or white flowers on compact plants to 12" tall; and **'Topknot,'** with large flowers in a similar range of colors held above the foliage on plants 12" tall.

I. walleriana with *Solenostemon* and *Ipomea batatas* (above), *I. balsamina* (below)

I. hawkeri New Guinea Hybrids (New Guinea Impatiens) grows 12–24" tall and 12" wide or wider. The flowers come in shades of red, orange, pink, purple or white. The foliage is often variegated with a yellow stripe down the center of each leaf. '**Tango**' is the most common variety to grow from seed. This compact plant grows 12–18" tall and wide and has orange flowers.

I. '**Seashell**' is a group of new African hybrids with flowers in shades of yellow, orange, apricot and pink. Plants grow 8–10" tall and spread about 12".

I. walleriana (Busy Lizzie) grows 6–18" tall and up to 24" wide. The flowers come in shades of red, orange, pink, purple or white, or are bicolored. '**Elfin**' series is a common group of cultivars. The flowers are available in many shades, including bicolors. The compact plants grow

about 12" tall, but they may spread more. '**Fiesta**' series bears double flowers in shades of pink, orange, red and burgundy. Compact plants grow about 12" tall, with an equal spread. With their habit and flower form, they resemble small rose bushes. '**Mosaic**' series has uniquely colored flowers, with the margins and most of the petals speckled in a darker shade of the petal color. '**Tempo**' series has a wide range of colors, including bicolors, and flowers with contrasting margins on the petals. '**Victoria Rose**' is an award-winning cultivar, with deep pink, double or semi-double flowers.

Problems & Pests

Fungal leaf spot, stem rot, *Verticillium* wilt, whiteflies and aphids can cause trouble.

I. walleriana

Lantana
Shrub Verbena
Lantana

Height: 18–24" **Spread:** up to 4' **Flower color:** yellow, orange, pink, purple, red, white; often in combination

THIS EASY-CARE PLANT WILL COLOR UP BORDERS AND CONTAINERS in the garden throughout the season. Its small clusters of flowers, which sport eye-catching combinations such as orange, yellow and pink, will act as magnets for butterflies. Lantana is one of the few annuals that is not stifled by hot, dry weather, and a 3" potted plant can reach the size of a small shrub in a single season. Lantana can be overwintered indoors, making it a good candidate for topiary and specimens.

Planting

Seeding: Start seed indoors in spring with soil temperature at 61°–64° F

Planting out: Into warm soil after danger of frost has passed

Spacing: 2–4'

Growing

Lantana grows best in **full sun** but tolerates partial shade. It prefers soil to be **fertile, moist** and **well drained** but can handle heat and drought.

Take cuttings in late summer if you would like to start plants for the following summer but don't want to store a large one over the winter.

Tips

Lantana is is a tender shrub that is grown as an annual. It is useful in beds and borders as well as in mixed containers and hanging baskets.

Lantana is rarely troubled by any pests or diseases and can handle hot weather, making it perfect for low-maintenance gardens.

Recommended

L. camara is a bushy plant that bears round clusters of flowers in many colors. 'Feston Rose' has flowers that open yellow and mature to bright pink. 'New Gold' bears clusters of bright yellow flowers. 'Radiation' has flowers that open yellow and mature to red. 'Spreading Sunset' bears brightly colored orange to red flowers.

'Spreading Sunset' (this page)

The flowers of Lantana often open one color and mature to a completely different color, creating a striking display as several colors may appear in a single cluster at once.

Larkspur
Rocket Larkspur, Annual Delphinium
Consolida (Delphinium)

Height: 1–4' **Spread:** 6–14" **Flower color:** blue, purple, pink, white

ONE OF MY FAVORITE FLOWERS, ANNUAL LARKSPUR MAKES A colorful addition to mixed borders, herb gardens, cottage gardens and wildflower plantings. If it likes its growing conditions, Larkspur will self-seed with abandon. The seeds need cool weather to germinate, so one of the secrets to growing this plant from seed is to sow as soon as the ground can be worked. Though we are told Larkspur is difficult to transplant, I have enjoyed great success growing transplants. The trick is to find a greenhouse that sells them.

Planting

Seeding: Indoors in mid-winter; direct sow in early or mid-spring, as soon as soil can be worked

Planting out: Mid-spring

Spacing: 12"

Growing

Larkspur does equally well in **full sun** or **light shade**. The soil should be **fertile,** rich in **organic matter** and **well drained**. Keep the roots cool and add a light mulch; dried grass clippings or shredded leaves work well. Don't put mulch too close to the base of the plant or the plant may develop crown rot.

Plant seeds in peat pots to prevent roots from being damaged when the plants are transplanted. Seeds started indoors may benefit from being chilled in the refrigerator for one week prior to sowing.

Deadhead to keep Larkspur blooming well into fall.

C. ajacis (all pictures)

Larkspur looks good at the back of a border, and its blooms make excellent cut flowers for arrangements.

Tips

Plant groups of Larkspur in mixed borders or cottage gardens. The tallest varieties may require staking to stay upright.

Recommended

C. ajacis *(C. ambigua, D. ajacis)* is an upright plant with feathery foliage. It bears spikes of purple, blue, pink or white flowers. **'Dwarf Rocket'** series includes plants that grow 12–20" tall and 6–10" wide and bloom in many colors. **'Earl Grey'** grows 3–4' tall and bears flowers in an intriguing color between slate gray

and gunmetal gray. **'Frosted Skies'** grows to 18" and bears large, semi-double flowers in a beautiful bicolor of blue and white. **'Giant Imperial'** series also comes in many colors. The plants grow 24–36" tall and up to 14" wide.

Problems & Pests

Slugs and snails are potential troublemakers. Powdery mildew and crown or root rot are avoidable if you water thoroughly, but not too often, and make sure the plants have good air circulation.

Lavatera
Mallow
Lavatera

Height: 20"–10' **Spread:** 18"–5' **Flower color:** pink, salmon, white, red, purple

CHANCES ARE YOU WON'T FIND THESE SHOWY COTTAGE-GARDEN bloomers in a garden center, so if you want to try them you will need to grow them from seed. The good news is that they are very easy to grow. Sow the seeds in the middle or back of the border as soon as the soil can be worked. Lavateras hate warm nights, so you may not see much of a show until late summer or early fall—but what a way to end the season! For me it's worth the wait to see those 4" hollyhock-like blooms cover the shrub-like plants when most other big bloomers are past their prime.

Planting

Seeding: Indoors in late winter; direct sow in spring

Planting out: After last frost

Spacing: 18–24"

Growing

Lavateras prefer **full sun**. The soil should be of **average fertility, light** and **well drained**. These plants like cool, moist weather. Select a site where the plants will be protected from wind exposure.

These plants resent having their roots disturbed when they are transplanted and tend to do better when sowed directly in the garden. If you choose to start seeds indoors, use peat pots.

L. t. 'Mont Blanc' (above), *L. t.* 'Silver Cup' (below)

Tips

Lavatera plants can be used as colorful backdrops behind smaller plants in a bed or border. The blooms make attractive cut flowers and are edible.

Lavateras grow to be fairly large and shrubby. Stake tall varieties to keep them from falling over in summer rain.

Recommended

L. arborea (Tree Mallow) is a large plant, capable of growing 10' tall and spreading 5'. The funnel-shaped flowers are pinkish purple.

Though there are only 25 species of Lavatera, *they are a diverse group comprising annuals, biennials, perennials and shrubs.*

L. t. 'Mont Blanc' (above), 'Silver Cup' (below)

The lifespan of this plant is undetermined. Typically grown as an annual, it can sometimes be treated as a biennial or perennial. The cultivar **'Variegata'** has cream-mottled leaves.

L. cachemiriana has light pink flowers. It can grow up to 8' tall and is usually half as wide. As the scientific name indicates, it is native to Kashmir.

L. trimestris is a bushy plant up to 4' tall and 18–24" wide. It bears red, pink or white, funnel-shaped flowers. **'Beauty'** series has plants in a variety of colors. **'Mont Blanc'** bears white flowers on compact plants that grow to about 20" tall. **'Silver Cup'** has cup-shaped light pink flowers with dark pink veins.

Problems & Pests

Plant lavateras in well-drained soil to avoid root rot. Destroy any rust-infected plants.

Lavateras are often called mallows, and they are in the same family as the true mallows (genus Malva).

L. t. 'Silver Cup' (above),
L. trimestris with *Verbena* (below)

Licorice Plant
False Licorice
Helichrysum

Height: 20" **Spread:** about 36"; sometimes up to 6' **Flower color:** yellow-white; plant grown for foliage

A DECADE AGO, AFTER A YEAR OF SEARCHING FOR THIS FABULOUS foliage plant, I finally found it at a farmers' market while vacationing in England. A lot has changed at garden centers since then, and I am pleased to say that Licorice Plant is now widely available. This vining subshrub makes an outstanding filler for large container plantings. Its elegant, velvety leaves complement and cool down strong colors. 'Limelight,' with its frosted chartreuse leaves, is a knockout paired with purple Heliotrope and 'Homestead Purple' verbena.

Planting
Seeding: Not recommended
Planting out: After last frost
Spacing: About 30"

Growing

Licorice Plant prefers **full sun.** The soil should be of **poor to average fertility, neutral or alkaline** and **well drained.** Licorice Plant wilts when the soil dries but revives quickly once watered. It is a rampant grower, but if it outgrows its space, a few snips with a pruner will quickly bring it back in line.

It is easy to start more plants from cuttings in fall for a supply of new plants the following spring. Once they have rooted, keep the young plants in a cool, bright room for winter.

Tips

Licorice Plant is a perennial grown as an annual. It is prized for its foliage rather than its flowers. Include it in your hanging baskets and container plantings, and the trailing growth will quickly fill in and provide a soft, silvery backdrop for the colorful flowers of other plants. Licorice Plant can also be used as an annual groundcover or as an edger in beds and borders. It will cascade down in a silvery wave over the rocks in rock gardens and along the tops of retaining walls.

This plant is a good indicator plant for hanging baskets. When you see Licorice Plant wilting, it is time to get out the hose or watering can.

Recommended

H. petiolare is a trailing plant with fuzzy gray-green leaves. Cultivars are more common than the species. 'Limelight' has bright lime green leaves that need protection from

H. petiolare cultivars (this page)

direct sun to maintain their color. 'Silver' is a common cultivar with gray-green leaves covered in a silvery down. 'Silver Spike' and 'Spike' are newer, upright cultivars. 'Variegatum,' a less common cultivar, has gray-green leaves dappled or margined in silvery cream.

Problems & Pests

Powdery mildew can be an occasional problem, though you might not see it because the leaves are already soft and white.

Lisianthus
Prairie Gentian
Eustoma

Height: 8–36" **Spread:** usually half the height **Flower color:** blue, purple, pink, yellow, white

AFTER ASKING THE NAME OF THE BEAUTIFUL CONTAINER PLANTS that graced the streets of Frankenmuth, Michigan, one of my readers was told it was 'Aunt Lizzie's Pants.' Well, that's one way to pronounce Lisianthus. Newer varieties are more tolerant than the species of hot weather, and giving them protection from the afternoon sun will help them succeed. Prized as cut flowers, these lovelies have an extended vase life that is appreciated by flower arrangers and florists. Seedlings take forever to mature, so it's best to buy Lisianthus as transplants.

Planting
Seeding: Indoors in early winter

Planting out: Mid-spring

Spacing: 4–12"

Growing

Lisianthus prefers **full sun** but in hot weather benefits from light or partial shade with protection from the afternoon sun. The soil should be of **average fertility** and **well drained**. A **neutral or alkaline** pH is preferred. If your soil is very acidic, grow the dwarf varieties in pots with an appropriate growing mix instead of struggling to keep Lisianthus healthy in the garden beds.

Seedlings can be quite slow to establish when seeds are sowed directly in the garden. It is best to start Lisianthus very early indoors with good light, or to purchase it at the garden center.

Tips

All varieties of Lisianthus look best grouped in flowerbeds or containers. The tallest varieties, with their long-lasting blooms, are popular in cut-flower gardens.

Recommended

E. grandiflora forms a slender, upright plant 24–36" tall, topped by satiny, cup-shaped flowers. 'Echo' series comes in many colors. Plants in this popular series are tall, to about 24", and they are admired for their double flowers that are perfect for fresh arrangements. 'Lisa' series also comes in many colors. This popular dwarf variety, which grows to about 8" tall, is reputed to bloom from seed one month sooner than other varieties.

A small vase filled with satin-textured Lisianthus flowers will add a touch of elegance to any table.

E. grandiflora (this page)

Problems & Pests

Generally, Lisianthus is trouble free; however, several diseases, including *Fusarium* wilt, can kill it. Purchase treated seed from a reputable source, and destroy any plants that appear diseased before the diseases have a chance to spread.

Livingstone Daisy
Ice Plant
Dorotheanthus (Mesembryanthemum)

Height: 6" **Spread:** 12" **Flower color:** pink, white, purple, crimson, orange, yellow or bicolored

THIS COLORFUL SUCCULENT SPORTS 2" WIDE, SPIDERY-PETALED, daisy-like flowers. The interesting, fleshy foliage is covered with small, ice-like lumps. More than drought tolerant, Livingstone Daisy requires minimal water to thrive. Situate it in spots around the garden where you would love a splash of color but where you rarely get around to watering.

Planting

Seeding: Indoors in late winter; direct sow in spring

Planting out: After last frost

Spacing: 12"

Growing

Livingstone Daisy likes to grow in **full sun**. The soil should be of **poor to average fertility, sandy** and **well drained**.

Tips

Brightly flowered and low growing, Livingstone Daisy can be used along edges of borders, on dry slopes, in rock gardens or in mixed containers. It can also be used between the stones or around the edges of a paved patio.

The flowers close on cloudy days.

D. bellidiformis (above), 'Lunette' (below)

Recommended

D. bellidiformis *(M. criniflorum)* is a low-growing, spreading plant. It bears brightly colored, daisy-like flowers. **'Lunette'** ('Yellow Ice') bears bright yellow flowers with red centers. **'Magic Carpet'** series has flowers in shades of purple, pink, white, yellow or orange. The petal bases are often lighter in color than the tips.

Problems & Pests

Slugs, snails and aphids may be troublesome.

Livingstone Daisy is also known as Ice Plant because of the tiny crystals that form on the leaves.

Lobelia
Edging Lobelia
Lobelia

Height: 4–10" **Spread:** equal to height **Flower color:** purple, blue, pink, white, red

LOBELIA ADDS BOTH COLOR AND FRILLS TO container plantings and border edgings, but she's a temperamental lady who hates hot weather. So when the days heat up, provide her with protection from the hot afternoon sun and keep her well watered or she will quickly decline. Shearing Lobelia plants back by one-third to one-half about two weeks before hot weather hits will tidy them up and may help them cope.

Planting
Seeding: Indoors in mid-winter

Planting out: After last frost

Spacing: 6"

Growing

Lobelia grows well in **full sun** or **partial shade**. The soil should be **fertile,** high in **organic matter, moist** and **fairly well drained.** Lobelia likes cool summer nights. In hot weather take care that its soil stays moist.

Lobelia seedlings are prone to damping off. See the 'Starting Annuals from Seed' section in the introduction to this book for information on proper propagation techniques to help avoid damping off.

Tips

Use Lobelia along the edges of beds and borders, on rock walls, in rock gardens, in mixed containers or in hanging baskets.

Trim Lobelia back after the first wave of flowers. It will stop blooming in the hottest part of summer but will usually revive in fall.

Recommended

L. erinus may be rounded and bushy or low and trailing. It bears flowers in shades of blue, purple, red, pink or white. **'Cascade'** series is a trailing form with flowers in many shades. **'Crystal Palace'** is a compact plant that rarely grows over 4" in height. This cultivar has dark green foliage and dark blue flowers. **'Regatta'** series is a trailing cultivar that tolerates heat better and blooms longer than other cultivars. **'Riviera'** series has flowers in blue and purple on bushy plants. **'Sapphire'** has white-centered blue flowers on trailing plants.

'Sapphire' (above), 'Cascade' (below)

Problems & Pests

Rust, leaf spot and slugs may be troublesome.

Love-in-a-Mist
Devil-in-a-Bush
Nigella

Height: 16–24" **Spread:** 8–12" **Flower color:** blue, white, pink, purple

IT AMAZES ME THAT MOTHER NATURE HAS MADE GROWING THIS lovely, exotic-looking flower almost effortless. Scatter the seeds about the garden and let the bloom-covered, fern-like foliage of this low grower fill in spaces between any slow-to-emerge perennials. The attractive seedheads, which quickly form once the petals drop, are prized for use in dried-flower arrangements, but to keep the flowers coming it's best to deadhead. Once established, Love-in-a-mist will self-sow, so do let some of the plants go to seed.

Planting

Seeding: Indoors in late winter; direct sow in early spring

Planting out: Mid-spring

Spacing: 10–15"

Growing

Love-in-a-mist prefers **full sun**. The soil should be of **average fertility, light** and **well drained.**

Direct sow seeds at two-week intervals all spring to prolong the blooming period. This plant resents having its roots disturbed. Seeds started indoors should be planted in peat pots or pellets to avoid damaging the roots when the plant is transplanted into the garden.

Love-in-a-mist has a tendency to self-sow and may show up in unexpected spots in your garden for years to come.

Tips

This attractive, airy plant is often used in mixed beds and borders. The flowers appear to float above the delicate foliage. The blooming may slow down and the plants may die back if the weather gets too hot for them during the summer.

The stems of this plant can be a bit floppy and may benefit from being staked with twiggy branches. Poke the branches in around the plants while they are young, and the plants will grow up between the twigs.

Recommended

N. damascena forms a loose mound of finely divided foliage. It grows 18–24" tall and spreads about half

N. damascena (this page)

this much. The light blue flowers darken as they mature. '**Miss Jekyll**' series bears semi-double flowers in rose pink, sky blue or a deep cornflower blue that pairs especially well with the golden yellow of coreopsis. Plants in this series grow to about 18" in height. '**Mulberry Rose**' bears light pink flowers that mature to dark pink. '**Persian Jewel**' series is one of the most common cultivars, with plants that usually grow to 16" tall and have flowers in many colors.

Marigold

Tagetes

Height: 7–36" **Spread**: 12–24" **Flower color:** yellow, red, orange, brown, gold, cream, bicolored

TWENTY YEARS AGO, MARIGOLDS WERE AS COMMON AS DUST IN Michigan gardens. Their popularity has declined in recent years, but if you need a tough flowering plant that can take the heat, take another look at marigolds. There are literally hundreds of varieties to choose from, and the inventive gardener can create a kaleidoscope of gold, orange, red, bronze and yellow by planting a mix of sizes and colors. Full sun is needed to keep disease at bay, and deadheading is a must to keep these plants in bloom. Tomato lovers who plant French Marigold to repel root nematodes should buy large transplants, because only the mature plants give off insecticidal compounds.

Planting

Seeding: Start indoors in spring or earlier

Planting out: Once soil has warmed

Spacing: Dwarf marigolds, 6"; tall marigolds, 12"

Growing

Marigolds grow best in **full sun**. The soil should be of **average fertility** and **well drained**. These plants are drought tolerant and hold up well in windy, rainy weather.

Remove spent blooms to encourage more flowers and to keep plants tidy.

Tips

Mass planted or mixed with other plants, marigolds make a vibrant addition to beds, borders and container gardens. These plants will thrive in the hottest, driest parts of your garden.

Recommended

T. erecta (African Marigold, American Marigold, Aztec Marigold) is 20–36" tall, with huge flowers. 'Cracker Jack' series bears large double flowers in bright shades of orange and yellow on tall plants up to 36" in height. 'Inca' bears double flowers in solid or multi-colored shades of yellow, gold and orange on compact plants that grow to 18" tall. 'Marvel' is another compact cultivar, growing only 18" tall, but with the large flowers that make the species popular. 'Vanilla' bears unique, cream white flowers on compact, odorless plants.

T. erecta (above), *T. patula* with annuals (below)

T. erecta and T. patula *are often used in vegetable gardens for their reputed insect-repelling qualities.*

T. patula (French Marigold) is low growing, only 7–10" tall. **'Bonanza'** series is a popular double-flowered cultivar. Its flowers are red, orange, yellow and bicolored. **'Janie'** series is another popular double-flowered cultivar. It is an early-blooming, compact plant with red, orange and yellow blooms.

T. tenuifolia (Signet Marigold) has dainty single flowers that grow on bushy plants with feathery foliage. **'Gem'** series is commonly available. The compact plants, about 10" tall, bear flowers in shades of yellow and orange, and the blooms last all summer. The flowers of plants in this series are edible.

***T*. Triploid Hybrids** (Triploid Marigold) have been developed by crossing *T. erecta* and *T. patula*.

T. patula (left), *T. tenuifolia* (below)

The resulting plants have the huge flowers of African Marigold and the compact growth of French Marigold. These hybrids are the most heat resistant of all the marigolds. They generally grow about 12" tall and spread 12–24". 'Nugget' bears large yellow, red, orange, gold or bicolored flowers on low, wide-spreading plants.

Problems & Pests

Slugs and snails can chew marigold seedlings to the ground.

When using marigolds as cut flowers, remove the lower leaves to take away some of the pungent scent.

T. erecta (above)

Mexican Sunflower

Tithonia

Height: 2–6' **Spread:** 12–24" **Flower color:** orange, red-orange, yellow

THE GLOWING ORANGE BLOSSOMS OF MEXICAN SUNFLOWER attract butterflies—and curious visitors wanting to know the name of this glorious flowering plant. Some Mexican Sunflower plants can reach up to 6' in height, so use these varieties only if you have lots of room. Crowding it will stress the plant and make it susceptible to aphids and other sucking insects. For smaller spaces, look for 'Fiesta del Sol,' an All-America winner that reaches only 30" in height.

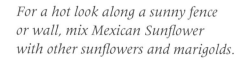

For a hot look along a sunny fence or wall, mix Mexican Sunflower with other sunflowers and marigolds.

Planting

Seeding: Indoors in early spring; direct sow in spring

Planting out: Once soil has warmed

Spacing: 12–24"

Growing

Mexican Sunflower grows best in **full sun.** The soil should be of **average to poor fertility** and **well drained.** Cover seeds lightly because they germinate more evenly and quickly when exposed to some light. Mexican Sunflower needs little water or care; however, it will bloom more profusely if it is deadheaded regularly.

Tips

Mexican Sunflower is heat resistant, so it is ideal for growing in a sunny, dry, warm spot such as under the eaves of a south-facing wall. The plants are tall and break easily if exposed to too much wind; grow along a wall or fence to provide shelter and stability. This annual has a coarse appearance and is well suited to the back of a border, where it will provide a good backdrop to a bed of shorter plants.

Recommended

T. rotundifolia is a vigorous, bushy plant. It grows 3–6' tall and spreads 12–24". Vibrant orange-red flowers are produced from mid- to late summer through to frost. 'Fiesta del Sol' bears bright orange flowers on plants that grow about 30" tall. 'Goldfinger' grows 24–36" tall and bears large orange flowers. 'Torch' has bright red-orange flowers. 'Yellow Torch' has bright yellow flowers.

Problems & Pests

This plant is generally resistant to most problems; however, young foliage may suffer slug and snail damage. Aphids can become a problem if not dealt with immediately.

Sear ends of cut flowers with a flame.

T. rotundifolia (below)

Million Bells
Calibrachoa
Calibrachoa

Height: 6–12" **Spread:** up to 24" **Flower color:** pink, purple, yellow, reddish orange, white, blue

THIS TINY RELATIVE OF PETUNIAS MADE ITS DEBUT IN EUROPE in the 1800s. But because Million Bells sets few seeds, propagating it was unprofitable and difficult. Thanks to the discovery of tissue culture, this dainty little powerhouse has come of age, and it's one of my favorites. With heavy-blooming, self-cleaning, compact growth that thrives in the sun, it's a stunner with staying power. Proven Winners offers 'Trailing Pink,' a true pink flower with a yellow throat. Allan Armitage recommends expanding your collection by rooting cuttings in damp potting soil. It's ever so easy, so give it a try.

Planting

Seeding: Seeds may not be available

Planting out: After last frost

Spacing: 6–15"

Growing

Million Bells prefers to grow in **full sun**. The soil should be **fertile, moist** and **well drained**. Though it prefers to be watered regularly, Million Bells is fairly drought resistant once established. It will bloom well into fall; the flowers become hardier as the weather cools and may survive temperatures down to 20° F.

'Cherry Pink' (above), 'Trailing Blue' and 'Trailing Pink' with *Heliotropium* (below)

Tips

Popular for planters and hanging baskets, Million Bells is also attractive in beds and borders. This plant grows all summer and needs plenty of room to spread or it will overtake other flowers. Pinch the flowers back to keep plants compact. In a hanging basket, it will produce plentiful bell-shaped blooms.

To protect the petals from rain, place hanging baskets under the eaves of the house or porch.

Recommended

Calibrachoa hybrids have a dense, trailing habit. They bear small, colorful, petunia-like flowers all summer. The **'Million Bells'** series includes **'Cherry Pink'** with reddish pink flowers on upright plants; **'Terracotta'** with reddish orange flowers and an upright habit; **'Trailing Blue'** with dark blue or purple, yellow-centered flowers; **'Trailing Pink'** with pink, yellow-centered flowers; **'Trailing White'** with white, yellow-centered flowers; and **'Yellow'** with bright yellow flowers.

Problems & Pests

Wet weather and cloudy days may cause leaf spot and delayed blooming. Watch for slugs that like to chew on the petals.

Monkey Flower

Mimulus

Height: 6–12" **Spread:** 12–24" **Flower color:** bright and pastel shades of orange, yellow, burgundy, pink, red, cream or bicolors

IF YOU'RE LOOKING FOR A FLOWERING ANNUAL THAT LIKES DAMP, partly shaded spots, give one of the monkey flowers a whirl. If the soil is kept moist, these plants will spend the summer covered with showy flowers. Monkey flowers make good container plants, and if well watered, these colorful bloomers can even be grown in full sun. They do, however, swoon as the summer heats up, so they are better placed where they will receive shade by early afternoon.

The cheerful blooms bring to mind a monkey's face, hence the common name. In a similar vein, the genus name, Mimulus, *means 'little actor' or 'little mime.'*

Planting

Seeding: Indoors in early spring

Planting out: Once soil warms after last frost

Spacing: 10–12"

Growing

Monkey flowers prefer **partial or light shade**. Protection from the afternoon sun will prolong the blooming of these plants. The soil should be **fertile, moist** and **humus rich**. Don't allow the soil to dry out. These plants can become scraggly and unattractive in hot sun.

Tips

Monkey flowers make an excellent addition to a border near a pond or to a bog garden. In a flowerbed, border or container garden, they will need to be watered regularly.

These plants are perennials that are grown as annuals. They can be over-wintered indoors in a cool, bright room.

Recommended

M. x *hybridus* is a group of upright plants with spotted flowers. They grow 6–12" tall and spread 12". 'Calypso' bears a mixture of flower colors. **'Mystic'** is compact and early flowering and offers a wide range of bright flower colors in solids or bicolors.

M. luteus (Yellow Monkey Flower), though not as common as the hybrids, is worth growing for its spreading habit and attractive yellow flowers. It grows about 12" tall

M. x *h.* 'Mystic' (this page)

and spreads up to 24". The yellow flowers are sometimes spotted with red or purple.

Problems & Pests

Downy or powdery mildew, gray mold, whiteflies, spider mites and aphids can cause occasional problems.

Morning Glory
Moonflower, Sweet Potato Vine, Mina Lobata
Ipomoea

Height: 6–15' **Spread:** 1–15' **Flower color:** white, blue, pink, red, yellow, orange, purple, sometimes bicolored

IT'S BEEN ALMOST A DECADE SINCE FLOWERING VINES CAME BACK in vogue in Michigan gardens, and their popularity continues to grow. The old-fashioned *I. tricolor* may be the best known of the *Ipomoea* group, but the related *I. alba* (Moonflower) and *I. batatas* (Sweet Potato Vine) are giving her a run for her money. If 'easy to grow' is your gardening mantra, any of the morning glories will please you.

Planting
Seeding: Indoors in early spring; direct sow after last frost

Planting out: Late spring

Spacing: 12–18"

Growing

Grow these plants in **full sun**. Any type of soil will do, but a **light, well-drained** soil of **poor to average fertility** is preferred. Moonflower needs warm weather to bloom.

These plants must twine around objects in order to climb them. Wide fence posts, walls or other broad objects must have a trellis or some wire or twine attached to them to provide the vines with something to grow on.

Soak seeds for 24 hours before sowing. If starting seeds indoors, sow them in individual peat pots.

I. tricolor (this page)

Tips

These vines can be grown anywhere: fences, walls, trees, trellises and arbors are all possible supports. As groundcovers, morning glories will grow over any obstacles they encounter. They can also be grown in hanging baskets.

If you have a bright sunny window, consider starting a hanging basket of morning glories indoors for a unique winter display. The vines will twine around the hangers and spill over the sides of the pot, providing you with beautiful trumpet flowers, regardless of the weather outside.

Each flower of a morning glory plant lasts only one day. The buds form a spiral that slowly unfurls as the day brightens with the rising sun.

Recommended

I. alba (Moonflower) has sweet-scented, white flowers that open only at night. It grows up to 15' tall.

Grow Moonflower on a trellis near a porch or patio that is used in the evenings, so that the sweetly scented flowers can be fully enjoyed. Once evening falls, the huge, white blossoms pour forth their sweet nectar, attracting night-flying moths.

I. alba (above), *I. b.* 'Blackie' with annuals (below)

*I. **batatas*** (Sweet Potato Vine) is a twining climber that is grown for its attractive foliage rather than its flowers. Often used in planters and hanging baskets, Sweet Potato Vine can be used by itself or mixed with other plants. It may spread or climb 10' or more in a summer. '**Blackie**' has dark purple (almost black), deeply lobed leaves. '**Marguerite**' ('Terrace Lime') has yellow-green foliage on fairly compact plants. This cascading plant can also be trained to grow up a trellis. As a bonus, when you pull up your plant at the end of summer, you can eat any tubers (sweet potatoes) that have formed on the roots.

*I. **lobata*** (Mina Lobata, Firecracker Vine, Exotic Love) is a twining climber 6–15' tall. The flowers are borne along one side of a spike. The buds are red and the flowers mature to orange then yellow, giving the spike a fire-like appearance.

*I. **tricolor*** (Morning Glory) is a twining climber that grows 10–12' tall in a single summer. There are many cultivars of this species available, although some listed as such may actually be cultivars of *I. nil.* '**Blue Star**' bears blue-and-white-streaked flowers. '**Heavenly Blue**' bears sky blue flowers with a white center.

Problems & Pests

Morning glories are susceptible to several fungal problems, but they occur only rarely.

Sweet Potato Vine is best recognized by its large, lime green, heart-shaped leaves, but the foliage is also available in shades of purple. Unlike the more aggressive morning glory species, Sweet Potato Vine doesn't twine or grasp or get carried away. Instead, it drapes politely over the sides of containers or spreads neatly over the soil beneath taller plants.

I. b. 'Blackie' (above), 'Marguerite' (below)

Moss Rose
Portulaca
Portulaca

Height: 4–8" **Spread:** 6–12" or more **Flower color:** red, pink, yellow, white, purple, orange, peach

IN MY MOTHER'S DAY, GARDENERS FACED WITH A DRY PLANTING space planted Moss Rose. That ground-hugging plant, with its small, rose-like blossoms, seemed to line the sides of every driveway. New varieties sport much larger flowers and make attractive additions to container plantings as well as rock gardens and cement-enclosed borders. For ground plantings, sandy or gravelly soil that drains like a sieve is a must, along with lots of sun.

Planting
Seeding: Indoors in late winter

Planting out: Once soil has warmed

Spacing: 12"

Growing

Moss Rose requires **full sun**. The soil should be of **poor fertility, sandy** and **well drained**. To ensure that you will have plants where you want them, start seed indoors. If you sow directly outdoors, the tiny seeds may get washed away by rain and the plants will pop up in unexpected places. Spacing the plants close together is not a problem; in fact, it results in well-mixed flower colors.

Tips

Moss Rose is the ideal plant for spots that just don't get enough water—under the eaves of the house or in dry, rocky, exposed areas. It is also ideal for people who like baskets hanging from the front porch but always forget to water them. As long as the location is sunny, this plant will do well with minimal care.

Recommended

P. grandiflora forms a bushy mound of succulent foliage. It bears delicate, papery, rose-like flowers profusely all summer. 'Cloudbeater' bears large double flowers in many colors. The flowers stay open all day, even in cloudy weather. 'Sundial' series has long-lasting double flowers. 'Sundial Peach' was an All-America winner; it has double flowers in shades of peach.

Problems & Pests

If Moss Rose has excellent drainage and as much light as possible, it shouldn't have problems.

P. grandiflora (this page)

Moss Rose will fill a sunny, exposed, narrow strip of soil next to pavement with bright colors all summer. It requires only minimal attention.

Nasturtium

Tropaeolum

Height: 12–18" for dwarf varieties; up to 10' for trailing varieties
Spread: equal to or slightly greater than height **Flower color:** red, orange,
yellow, burgundy, pink, cream, gold, white or bicolored

THE MOST FAMOUS CHAMPION OF THE COMMON NASTURTIUM
was none other than the painter Claude Monet. He lined the borders of his
alley and the entrance to his home in the south of France with
these colorful trailers, and by mid-summer they almost
enveloped the walk with a colorful carpet of red and green.
Nasturtiums are a snap for even the most inexperienced gardener to grow, as these plants thrive on neglect.

Planting

Seeding: Indoors in late winter; direct sow around last frost date

Planting out: After last frost

Spacing: 12"

Growing

Nasturtiums prefer **full sun** but tolerate some shade. The soil should be of **average to poor fertility, light, moist** and **well drained**. Too rich a soil or too much nitrogen fertilizer will result in lots of leaves and very few flowers. Let the soil drain completely between waterings.

If you start nasturtium seeds indoors, sow them in individual peat pots to avoid disturbing the roots during transplanting.

Tips

Nasturtiums are used in beds and borders, in containers and hanging baskets and on sloped banks. The climbing varieties are grown up trellises or over rock walls or places that need concealing. These plants thrive in poor locations, and they make an interesting addition to plantings on hard-to-mow slopes.

Some gardeners believe that nasturtiums attract and harbor certain pests, such as whiteflies and aphids, and that they should not be grown near plants that are susceptible to the same problems. Other gardeners believe that nasturtiums are preferred by pest insects and that the pests will flock to them and leave the rest of the garden alone. Still other gardeners claim that these plants, because of the high sulfur

'Alaska' (above), *T. majus* (below)

RECIPE
Poor Man's Capers
(Pickled Nasturtium Seedpods)

1. Soak green seedpods for 24 hours in a brine made from 2 cups of water and 1 tbsp. salt.

2. Pack small, sterilized jars with the seedpods, one peeled clove of garlic and 1 tsp. pickling spices.

3. Heat white wine vinegar to simmering and fill each jar with the vinegar.

4. Seal with acid-proof lids and let the seedpods sit for about a month.

The pickled seedpods should be eaten within a week of opening.

levels in the leaves, repel many pests that would otherwise infest the garden. Whatever the case, if you do find aphids on the plants, you will notice that they congregate near the growing tips. Cut the infested parts off and drop them in a bucket of soapy water to rid yourself of this problem.

Recommended

T. majus has a trailing habit. It has been greatly improved by hybridizing. The foliage of the older varieties tended to hide the flowers, but new varieties hold their flowers (available in a great selection of colors) above the foliage. There are also some new and interesting cultivars with variegated foliage and compact, attractive, mound-forming habits. 'Alaska' series has white-marbled foliage. 'Jewel' series has compact plants that grow to 12" tall and wide, with

T. majus (below)

double flowers in a mix of deep orange, red or gold. **'Peach Melba'** forms a 12" mound. The flowers are pale yellow with a bright orange-red splash at the base of each petal. **'Whirlybird'** is a compact, bushy plant. The single or double flowers in shades of red, pink, yellow or orange do not have spurs.

Problems & Pests

The few problems that afflict nasturtiums include aphids, slugs, whiteflies and some viruses.

Nasturtiums have a place in any vegetable or herb garden. The leaves and flowers are edible and can be added to salads, soups and dips. They have a peppery flavor, so don't overdo it. The unripe seedpods can be pickled and used as a substitute for capers.

'Peach Melba' (above), 'Alaska' (below)

Nemesia

Nemesia

Height: 6–24" **Spread:** 4–12" **Flower color:** red, blue, purple, pink, white, yellow, orange or bicolored

THE TINY, ORCHID-LIKE FLOWERS OF THESE SOUTH AFRICAN natives make a lovely addition to container gardens. 'Blue Bird' and 'Compact Innocence' have been bred to stand up to both hot and cool weather and are available as transplants. One secret to success in growing nemesias is to keep them well watered. Mix them with heat-tolerant plants such as hot pink 'Temari' verbenas, so that if an extended heat wave proves too much for the nemesias, the other plants will keep color coming.

Planting

Seeding: Start indoors in early spring

Planting out: After last frost

Spacing: 6"

Growing

Nemesias prefer **full sun**. The soil should be **average to fertile, slightly acidic, moist** and **well drained**. Regular watering will keep these plants blooming through the summer.

Tips

Nemesias make a bright and colorful addition to the front of a mixed border or mixed container planting.

Recommended

N. caerulea (*N. fruticans*) is a perennial that is sometimes grown as an annual. This bushy plant grows up to 24" tall and spreads about 12". It bears blue, pink, purple or white flowers. Several cultivars are available as transplants. **'Bluebird'** bears lavender blue flowers on plants 8–12" tall. **'Compact Innocence'** bears white flowers.

N. strumosa cultivars (this page)

N. strumosa forms a bushy mound of bright green foliage. It grows 6–12" tall and spreads 4–8". It bears flowers in shades of blue, purple, white, pink, red or yellow, often in bicolors. **'Carnival'** series bears many flowers in yellow, white, orange, pink or red on compact plants. **'KLM'** has bicolored blue and white flowers with yellow throats. **'National Ensign'** ('Red and White') bears flowers bicolored red and white.

Problems & Pests

Occasional problems with crown or root rot are possible.

Nicotiana
Flowering Tobacco Plant
Nicotiana

Height: 1–5' **Spread:** 12" **Flower color:** red, pink, purple, green, yellow, white

THESE COLORFUL MEMBERS OF THE TOBACCO FAMILY HAVE become popular additions to Michigan gardens in recent years. The compact series 'Nicki' and 'Domino' are self-cleaning and require little maintenance other than regular watering to keep their soil moist. For a conversation piece, consider *N. langsdorffii*, a 3–5' species that produces attention-getting sprays of apple green, bell-shaped flowers. For interest and intense fragrance, the tall *N. sylvestris* can't miss.

Planting

Seeding: Indoors in early spring; direct sow once soil warms

Planting out: Once soil has warmed

Spacing: 8–12"

Growing

Nicotianas grow equally well in **full sun, light shade** or **partial shade.** The soil should be **fertile,** high in **organic matter, moist** and **well drained.**

The seeds require light for germination, so leave them uncovered.

N. alata (above),
Photo (below) showing *N. sylvestris* (top), *Cleome,* and *N. alata* 'Nicki' (bottom)

Tips

Nicotianas are popular in beds and borders. The dwarf varieties do well in containers. Do not plant nicotianas near tomatoes because, as members of the same plant family, they share a vulnerability to many of the same diseases. The nicotiana plant may attract and harbor diseases that will hardly affect it but that can kill tomatoes.

Recommended

N. alata is an upright plant that grows up to 5' tall and has a strong, sweet fragrance. '**Domino**' series is compact and plants grow 12–18" tall with an equal spread. Flowers come in many colors and stay open all day. '**Merlin**' series has dwarf plants ideal for mixed planters. The flowers may be red, pink, purple, white or pale green. '**Nicki**' series has fragrant blooms in many colors, and the flowers stay open all day. The compact plants grow up to 18" tall. '**Only the Lonely**' grows up to 4' tall and bears white blooms

that give off a scent in the evening. 'Sensation' grows up to 30" tall and bears red, white or pink flowers that stay open all day.

N. langsdorffii grows up to 3–5' tall. It bears clusters of green flowers. The leaves and stems are hairy and feel sticky to the touch.

N. '**Lime Green**' produces green, star-like flowers on upright plants that grow to 30" tall.

N. sylvestris grows up to 4' tall and bears white blooms that give off a scent in the evening.

Problems & Pests

Tobacco mosaic virus, aphids and downy or powdery mildew may cause occasional problems.

N. alata (above & below), 'Nicki' (below right)

Nicotianas were originally cultivated for the wonderful scent of the flowers. The first plants had green flowers that opened only in the evening and at night. In attempts to expand the variety of colors and the daily blooming period, the popular scent has sometimes been lost.

N. sylvestris (above)

Painted-Tongue
Velvet Flower
Salpiglossis

Height: up to 24" **Spread:** 12" **Flower color:** red, yellow, orange, pink, purple; often patterned bicolors

THE GORGEOUS FLOWERS OF PAINTED-TONGUE, WHICH IS RELATED to morning glories and nicotianas, must be seen to be fully appreciated. But if you believe that beauty is as beauty does when it comes to flowers, you may want to think twice about growing this lovely. It can't take the heat and is easily shredded by wind and rain. If, on the other hand, you are an adventurous sort who likes to try new things, and if you are happy to experience a potentially fleeting burst of dramatic beauty, grow Painted-tongue and enjoy.

Planting

Seeding: Indoors in late winter; direct sow in spring

Planting out: After last frost

Spacing: 12"

Growing

Painted-tongue prefers **full sun**. The soil should be **fertile**, rich in **organic matter** and **well drained**.

The seeds are very tiny and shouldn't be covered with soil. They will germinate more evenly if kept in darkness until they sprout: place pots in a dark closet or cover pots with dark plastic or layers of newspaper. Once they start to sprout, the plants can be moved to a well-lit location.

Tips

Painted-tongue is useful in the middle or back of beds and borders. It can also be added to large mixed containers. Most types of Painted-tongue can become battered in rain and wind, so plant in a warm, sheltered area of the garden.

The iridescent quality of these flowers causes their color to change as they turn in a breeze.

Recommended

S. sinuata is an upright plant in the same family as petunias. 'Blue Peacock' has blue flowers with yellow throats and dark veins. Plants of the 'Casino' series, with flowers in a wide range of colors, bloom early and tolerate rain and wind.

Problems & Pests

Occasional problems with aphids or root rot are possible.

Passion Flower

Passiflora

Height: up to 30' **Spread:** variable **Flower color:** white or pale pink petals with blue or purple bands

TRULY EXOTIC IS THE ONLY WAY TO DESCRIBE THE BLOOMS OF Passion Flower. Once a rare bird that could be grown only from seed, the vine is now fairly easy to find in garden centers. Fertilize sparingly because too much nitrogen will result in lots of foliage and no flowers. If planted as a small seedling, the vine may not flower the first year and will need to be over-wintered indoors.

Planting

Seeding: Not recommended

Planting out: Several weeks after the last frost

Spacing: 12"

Growing

Grow Passion Flower in **full sun** or **partial shade**. This plant prefers **well-drained, moist** soil of average fertility. Keep it sheltered from wind and cold.

Germination is erratic and propagation is generally easier from cuttings, but for gardeners who like a challenge, it is possible to propagate Passion Flower from seed. Soak seeds for 24 hours in hot water before planting. Place the seed tray in full sun because the seeds need light to germinate. Keep the soil moist and at about 59° F.

Tips

Passion Flower is a popular addition to mixed containers and makes an unusual focal point near a door or other entryway. This plant is actually a fast-growing woody climber that is grown as an annual.

The common name refers not to physical love but to Christ's Passion. The three stigmas of the flower are said to represent the nails and the five anthers the wounds.

Many garden centers now sell small Passion Flower plants in spring. They quickly climb trellises and other supports over summer. They can be composted at the end of summer or cut back and brought inside to enjoy in a bright room over winter.

The small round fruits are edible but not very tasty.

Recommended

P. caerulea (Blue Passion Flower) bears unusual purple-banded, purple-white flowers all summer. 'Constance Elliott' bears fragrant white flowers.

Problems & Pests

Spider mites, whiteflies, scale insects and nematodes may cause occasional trouble.

Periwinkle
Madagascar Periwinkle
Catharanthus

Height: 12–24" **Spread:** usually equal to or greater than height
Flower color: red, rose, pink, mauve, apricot or white,
often with contrasting centers

THIS LITTLE BLOOMER IS AN OLD FAVORITE THAT HAS UNDERGONE
real improvement by hybridizers, resulting in larger blossoms and a wider variety
of colors. But to grow it successfully, you must remember that it needs fast-
draining soil and enjoys being drenched in hot sun. Given those conditions it
will bloom throughout the growing season with little attention. As a bonus, the
spent flowers fall freely, so deadheading is not necessary.

Planting

Seeding: Indoors in mid-winter

Planting out: After last frost

Spacing: 8–18"

Growing

Periwinkle prefers **full sun** but tolerates partial shade. Any **well-drained** soil is fine. This plant tolerates pollution and drought but prefers to be watered regularly. It doesn't like to be too wet or too cold. Plant Periwinkle after the soil has warmed because it may not thrive in cold, wet soil.

Keep seedlings warm and take care not to overwater them. The soil temperature should be 55°–64° F for seeds to germinate.

Tips

Periwinkle will do well in the sunniest, warmest part of the garden. Plant it in a bed along an exposed driveway or against the south-facing wall of the house. It can also be used in hanging baskets, in planters and as a temporary groundcover.

This plant is a perennial that is grown as an annual. In a bright room, it can be grown as a houseplant.

Recommended

C. roseus (Vinca rosea) forms a mound of strong stems. The flowers are pink, red or white, often with contrasting centers. 'Apricot Delight' bears pale apricot flowers with bright raspberry red centers. 'Cooler' series has light-colored flowers with darker, contrasting centers. 'Pacifica' has flowers in various colors on compact plants.

Problems & Pests

Slugs can be troublesome. Most rot and other fungal problems can be avoided by not overwatering.

One of the best annuals to use in front of homes on busy streets, Periwinkle will bloom happily despite exposure to exhaust fumes and dust.

Persian Shield

Strobilanthes

Height: 18–36" **Spread:** 24–36" **Flower color:** blue; plant grown for green, purple and silver foliage

COLORFUL FOLIAGE IS WHAT THIS PLANT IS ALL ABOUT. BRONZE leaves frosted with purplish pink and finished with a silver glaze add a dramatic touch to container gardens. In summer, Persian Shield produces tiny, blue flowers that are of little consequence; clip them off so they don't distract. If given ample water and afternoon shade in the heat of summer, this plant will burgeon to 36" in height. Persian Shield is a perennial in Zone 10, and you can try taking root cuttings in late summer to color up the indoor garden.

Planting

Seeding: Not recommended

Planting out: In warm soil after last frost

Spacing: 24"

Growing

Persian Shield grows well in **full sun** and **partial shade**. The soil should be **average to fertile, light** and very **well drained**. Pinch growing tips to encourage bushiness.

Tips

The colorful foliage provides a dramatic background in annual or mixed borders and in container plantings. Combine with yellow- or white-flowered plants for a stunning contrast.

Recommended

S. dyerianus is a tender shrub that is grown as an annual. It forms a bushy mound of silver- or purple-flushed foliage with contrasting dark

green or purple veins and margins. The foliage emerges purple and matures to silver. Plants may produce spikes of blue flowers in early fall.

Problems & Pests

Trouble with root rot is possible in very wet soils.

Petunia
Petunia

Height: 6–18" **Spread:** 12–24" or more **Flower color:** pink, purple, red, white, yellow, coral, blue or bicolored

IF PINCHING, PRUNING AND DEADHEADING ARE NOT YOUR THING, you may have turned your nose up at petunias back in the '80s. Well, these babies have come a long way since then. Thanks to the introduction of wonderful new varieties, such as 'Supercascade,' 'Surfinia' and 'Wave,' they are destined to again outrank impatiens as America's most popular bedding plant. Their compact growth, tolerance of wet weather and self-cleaning habit make them easy to care for. Neon bright to sherbet subtle, singles or doubles, large or small, there's a flower here for every taste.

The name Petunia is derived from petun, *the Brazilian word for tobacco, which comes from species of the related* genus Nicotiana.

Planting

Seeding: Indoors in mid-winter

Planting out: After last frost

Spacing: 12–18"

Growing

Petunias prefer **full sun**. The soil should be of **average to rich fertility, light, sandy** and **well drained**. When sowing, press seeds into the soil surface but don't cover them with soil. Pinch halfway back in mid-summer to keep plants bushy and to encourage new growth and flowers.

Tips

Use petunias in beds, borders, containers and hanging baskets.

Recommended

P. x hybrida is a large group of popular, sun-loving annuals that fall into three categories: grandifloras, multifloras and millifloras.

The **grandiflora** petunias have the largest flowers—up to 4" across. They have the widest variety of colors and forms, but they are the most likely to be damaged by heavy rain. '**Daddy**' series is available in darkly veined shades of pink and purple. '**Supercascade**' series comes in a wide variety of colors. '**Ultra**' series is available in many colors, including bicolors. This cultivar recovers quite quickly from weather damage.

Compared to the grandifloras, the **multiflora** petunias have smaller blooms (about half the size), bear many more flowers and tolerate adverse weather conditions better.

Milliflora variety (below)

'Carpet' series is available in a wide variety of colors. 'Surfinia' series plants branch freely, are self-cleaning and form a neat mound covered by a mass of flowers in shades of pink, blue, purple and white. Look for new additions to the series, which feature double flowers, minis, pastel colors and decorative veining. 'Wave' series is available in pink, purple and coral. The low, spreading habit makes this series popular as a groundcover and for hanging baskets and containers. The plants recover well from rain damage, bloom nonstop, tolerate cold and spread quickly.

'Purple Wave' (above), 'Fantasy' (below)

The **milliflora** petunias are the newest group. The flowers are about 1" across and are borne profusely over the whole plant. These plants tolerate wet weather very well and sometimes self-seed. They are popular in mixed containers and hanging baskets and are also very nice in garden beds, forming neat mounds of foliage and flowers. '**Fantasy**' series is available in shades of red, purple, pink and white, although the pinks tend to be easiest to find. With the growing popularity of the millifloras, more colors will likely become available.

Problems & Pests

Aphids and fungi may present problems. Fungal problems can be avoided by wetting the foliage as little as possible and by providing a location with good drainage.

Grandiflora variety (above), 'Lavender Wave' (below)

Phlox

Phlox

Height: 6–18" **Spread:** 10" or more **Flower color:** purple, pink, red, blue, white, yellow

ANNUAL PHLOX COMES IN A SPLENDID ARRAY OF COLORS, AND although it is not terribly heat tolerant, it is the quintessential cottage-garden flower. Phlox mixes nicely with trailing verbenas and blue and white Mealy Cup Sage in the garden, and if it falters, the verbenas will quickly fill the space. Start Phlox seed again in mid-summer to enjoy late-summer and fall blooms.

Planting

Seeding: Direct sow in early spring and mid-summer

Spacing: Up to 8"

Growing

Phlox prefers **full sun**. The soil should be **fertile, moist** and **well drained**. This plant resents being transplanted, and starting it indoors is not recommended. Germination takes 10–15 days. Phlox can be propagated from cuttings and will root easily in moist soil. Plants can be spaced quite close together. Deadhead to promote blooming.

Tips

Use Phlox on rock walls and in beds, borders, containers and rock gardens.

P. drummondii (this page)

Recommended

P. drummondii forms a bushy plant that can be upright or spreading. It bears clusters of white, purple, pink or red flowers. **'Coral Reef'** bears attractive pastel-colored flowers. **'Twinkle'** mixed has unusual small, star-shaped flowers on compact plants 8" tall. The colors of the petal margins and centers often contrast with the main petal color.

Problems & Pests

To avoid fungal problems, provide good drainage and don't let water stand on the leaves late in the day. Water the plants in the morning during dry spells and avoid handling wet foliage.

P. drummondii is a Texan species of Phlox that is named for Thomas Drummond (1790–1835), who collected plants in North America.

Poppy

Shirley Poppy, Corn Poppy, Flanders Poppy
Papaver

Height: 1–4' **Spread:** 12" **Flower color:** red, pink, white, purple, yellow, orange

FLOWERING IN SPRING AND EARLY SUMMER, ANNUAL POPPIES ARE colorful harbingers of the new gardening season. Sow the seeds as soon as the soil can be worked, and within weeks your garden will be awash with bright colors or blushing pastels. These fleeting showmen will not interfere with later-blooming perennials, so just remove the spent plants as they decline to make way for the next act.

Planting

Seeding: Direct sow every two weeks in spring

Spacing: 12"

Growing

Poppies grow best in **full sun**. The soil should be **fertile** and **sandy** and have lots of **organic matter** mixed in. **Good drainage** is essential. Do not start seeds indoors because transplanting is often unsuccessful. Mix the tiny seeds with fine sand for even sowing. Do not cover, because seeds need light for germination. Deadhead to prolong blooms.

Tips

Poppies work well in mixed borders where other plants are slow to fill in. Poppies will fill in empty spaces early in the season then die back over the summer, leaving room for other plants. They can also be used in rock gardens, and the cut flowers are popular for fresh arrangements.

Be careful when weeding around faded summer plants; you may accidentally pull up germinating poppy seedlings.

P. somniferum (above), *P. nudicaule* (below)

The seeds of both Shirley Poppy and Opium Poppy can be used to flavor baked goods such as muffins, breads and bagels.

P. somniferum (above), *P. rhoeas* (below)

Recommended

P. nudicaule (Iceland Poppy) is a short-lived perennial that is grown as an annual. It grows 12–18" tall and spreads about 12". Red, orange, yellow, pink or white flowers appear in spring and early summer. This plant tends to self-seed, but it will gradually disappear from the garden if left to its own devices. '**Champagne Bubbles**' bears flowers in solid and bicolored shades of red, orange and yellow.

P. rhoeas (Flanders Poppy, Field Poppy, Corn Poppy) forms a basal rosette of foliage above which the flowers are borne on long stems. '**Mother of Pearl**' bears flowers in pastel pinks and purples. '**Shirley**' series (Shirley Poppy) has silky, cup-shaped petals. The flowers come in many colors and may be single, semi-double or double.

P. somniferum (Opium Poppy) grows up to 4' tall. The flowers are red, pink, white or purple. This plant has a mixed reputation. Its milky sap is the source of several drugs, including codeine, morphine and opium. All parts of the plant can cause stomach upset and even coma except for the seeds, which are a popular culinary additive (poppy seeds). The seeds contain only minute amounts of the chemicals that make this plant pharmaceutically valuable. The large seed capsules are also dried and used in floral arrangements. Though propagation of the species is restricted in many countries, several attractive cultivars have been developed for ornamental use. '**Danebrog Lace**' originated in the 19th century. The single flowers have frilly red petals with a large white patch at the base of each petal. **'Peony Flowered'** has large, frilly double flowers in a variety of colors on plants that grow up to 36" tall.

Problems & Pests

Poppies rarely have problems, although fungi may be troublesome if the soil is wet and poorly drained.

For cut flowers, seal the cut end of each stem with a flame or boiling water.

P. rhoeas (this page)

Salvia
Sage
Salvia

Height: 1–4' **Spread:** 8"–4' **Flower color:** red, blue, purple, burgundy, pink, orange, salmon, yellow, cream, white or bicolored

IF YOU'VE DISMISSED SALVIAS AS 'THE RED FLOWERS they always plant around gas stations,' you're missing out. New cultivars, such as the 'Salsa' series and 'Sizzler' series, in luscious shades of burgundy, lavender, salmon and cream, make colorful additions to container gardens, beds and borders. Their long-lasting flowers hold up in the worst weather, making them delightfully easy to care for. Occasional deadheading is all that's required. If you're mad for blue, add 'Victoria' to the garden for season-long color.

The genus name Salvia *comes from the Latin* salvus, *'save,' referring to the medicinal properties of several species.*

Planting

Seeding: Indoors in mid-winter; direct sow in spring

Planting out: After last frost

Spacing: 10"

Growing

All salvias prefer **full sun** but tolerate light shade. The soil should be **moist, well drained** and of **average to rich fertility,** with lots of **organic matter.**

To keep plants producing flowers, water often and fertilize monthly. Remove spent flowers before they begin to turn brown.

Tips

Salvias look good grouped in beds, borders and containers. The flowers are long lasting and make lovely cut flowers for arrangements.

S. splendens (above), *S. f.* 'Victoria' with *Tanacetum, Rudbeckia* and *Platycodon* (below)

S. elegans (above), S. farinacea (below)

Recommended

S. argentea (Silver Sage) is grown for its large, fuzzy, silvery leaves. It grows up to 36" tall, spreads about 24" and bears small white or pink-tinged flowers. This plant is a short-lived perennial grown as an annual.

S. elegans *(S. rutilans)* (Pineapple Sage) is a large, bushy plant with soft leaves and bright red flowers. It grows 3–4' tall, with an equal spread. The foliage smells of pineapple when crushed and is used as a culinary flavoring.

S. farinacea (Mealy Cup Sage, Blue Sage) has bright blue flowers clustered along stems powdered with silver. The plant grows up to 24" tall, with a spread of 12". The flowers are also available in white. '**Victoria**' is a popular cultivar with silvery foliage and deep blue flowers that make a beautiful addition to cut-flower arrangements.

S. patens (Gentian Sage) bears vivid blue flowers on plants 18–24" tall. This is a tender perennial grown as an annual. Being tuberous-rooted, it can be lifted and brought inside for the winter in the same way as dahlias. '**Cambridge Blue**' bears pale blue flowers.

S. splendens (Salvia, Scarlet Sage) grows 12–18" tall and spreads up to 12". It is known for its spikes of bright red, tubular flowers. Recently, cultivars have become available in white, pink, purple and orange. '**Phoenix**' forms neat, compact plants with flowers in many bright and pastel shades. '**Salsa**' bears solid and bicolored flowers in shades of red, orange, purple, burgundy, cream and pink. **'Sizzler'** series bears flowers in burgundy, lavender, pink, plum, red, salmon, and white and salmon bicolor. **'Vista'** is an early-flowering, compact plant with dark blue-green foliage and bright red flowers.

S. viridis (S. horminum) (Annual Clary Sage) is grown for its colorful bracts, not its flowers. It grows 18–24" tall, with a spread of 8–12". **'Claryssa'** grows 18" tall and has bracts in pink, purple, blue or white. **'Oxford Blue'** bears purple-blue bracts.

Problems & Pests

Seedlings are prone to damping off. Aphids and a few fungal problems may occur.

S. viridis *(pictured above) has been used externally to relieve sore gums. It has also been used as snuff and as flavoring for beers and wines.*

Scabiosa
Pincushion Flower
Scabiosa

Height: 18–36" **Spread:** up to 12" **Flower color:** purple, blue, maroon, pink, white, red

THE ANNUAL SPECIES OF SCABIOSA MAY BE NEW TO YOU, BUT they've been around for ages. The flowers are almost identical to those of the perennial species but come in a wider range of colors and are often double. The blooms make long-lived cut flowers as well as colorful additions to beds and borders. They blend well into wildflower or cottage gardens.

Planting
Seeding: Indoors in late winter; direct sow in mid-spring

Planting out: After last frost

Spacing: 12–16"

Growing

Scabiosas grow best in **full sun**. The soil should be of **average to rich fertility, alkaline, well drained** and rich in **organic matter**. Keep soil moderately moist, but do not overwater.

Tips

Scabiosas are useful in beds, borders and mixed containers. The flowers are also popular in fresh arrangements.

The tall stems of *S. atropurpurea* may fall over as the plants mature. Insert twiggy branches, called pea sticks, into the ground around the plants when they are small to give them support as they grow.

Recommended

S. atropurpurea is an upright, branching plant growing up to 36" tall and spreading about 12". Its flowers may be white, blue, purple or red. 'Imperial Giants' bears blooms in a deep maroon color as well as shades of pink.

S. stellata grows 18" tall and spreads half as much. This plant bears small white flowers but is grown for its papery, orb-like seedpods, which dry in unusual globe shapes and are useful accents in dried arrangements. Pick *S. stellata* while still slightly green to keep the dried seedpods from shattering. 'Paper Moon' ('Drumstick') bears blue flowers that dry to a warm bronze color.

Scabiosas blend well into a wildflower or a cottage garden.

S. atropurpurea (this page)

The rounded, densely petaled blooms serve as a perfect landing pad for butterflies.

Snapdragon
Antirrhinum

Height: 6"–4' **Spread:** 6–24" **Flower color:** white, cream, yellow, orange, red, maroon, pink, purple or bicolored

MOTHER NATURE WAS HAVING A GOOD DAY when she created snapdragons. Gardeners of all ages love to make magic with these flowers, which look like delightful, tiny dragon heads. The tall, pink 'Rocket' snapdragons mimic the foxgloves in my perennial garden, and the short upright and trailing varieties make lovely additions to container gardens. Snaps can handle cold weather, so they are a good choice for those who like to tempt fate and plant their annuals before the last-frost date.

Planting

Seeding: Indoors in late winter; direct sow in spring

Planting out: After last frost

Spacing: 6–18"

Snapdragons are interesting and long lasting in fresh flower arrangements. The buds will continue to mature and open even after the spike is cut from the plant.

Growing

Snapdragons prefer **full sun** but tolerate light or partial shade. The soil should be **fertile**, rich in **organic matter** and **well drained**. Snapdragons prefer a **neutral or alkaline** soil and will not perform as well in acidic soil. Do not cover seeds when sowing because they require light for germination.

To encourage bushier growth, pinch the tips of the plants while they are young. Cut off the flower spikes as they fade to promote further blooming and to prevent the plant from dying back before the end of the season.

A. majus cultivars (all pictures)

Tips

The height of the variety dictates the best place for it in a border—the shortest varieties work well near the front, and the tallest look good in

Snapdragons may self-sow but the hybrids will not come true to type, so unless you enjoy experimenting you might wish to pull the seedlings out.

the center or back. The dwarf and medium-height varieties can also be used in planters, and there is even a trailing variety that does well in hanging baskets.

Snapdragons are perennials grown as annuals; they can tolerate cold nights well into fall and may survive a mild winter. Self-sowed seedlings may sprout the following spring if plants are left in place over winter, but because most snapdragons are hybrids they will not come true to form.

Recommended

Many cultivars of *A. majus* are available. Snapdragons are grouped into three sizes: dwarf, medium and giant.

Dwarf varieties grow up to 12" tall. 'Floral Showers' is a true dwarf, growing 6–8" tall. This plant bears flowers in a wide range of solid colors and bicolors. 'Lampion' is a new and interesting cultivar, usually grouped with the semi-dwarfs. It has a trailing habit and cascades up to 36", making it a great plant for hanging baskets. 'Princess' bears white and purple bicolored flowers. This plant produces many shoots from the base and therefore many flower spikes.

Medium snapdragons grow 12–24" tall. 'Black Prince' bears striking, dark purple-red flowers set against bronze-green foliage. 'Sonnet' series grows to 36" in height and is as attractive as a cut flower as it is in the garden.

Giant cultivars can grow 3–4' tall. 'Madame Butterfly' bears double flowers in a wide range of colors. The flowers of this cultivar are open-faced with a ruffled edge and they don't 'snap,' because the hinged, mouth-like structure has been lost with the addition of the extra petals. 'Rocket' series produces long spikes of brightly colored flowers in many shades and has good heat tolerance.

Problems & Pests

Snapdragons can suffer from several fungal problems, including powdery mildew, fungal leaf spot, root rot, wilt and downy mildew. Snapdragon rust is the worst. To prevent rust, avoid wetting the foliage when watering, choose varieties that are rust resistant and plant snapdragons in different parts of the garden each year. Aphids may also be troublesome.

Statice
Limonium

Height: 12–24" **Spread:** 6–12" **Flower color:** blue, purple, pink, white, yellow, red, orange

THIS POPULAR EVERLASTING, ONCE RELEGATED TO THE DRIED-flower grower's garden, is making a name for itself in decorative gardens. Statice makes an attractive temporary hedge in dry areas of the landscape where color is often hard to come by. Combine it with other drought-tolerant annuals, such as Baby's Breath, Bachelor's Buttons and the verbenas, to fill in and add color to a neglected corner of the garden.

Planting

Seeding: Indoors in mid-winter; direct sow in spring

Planting out: After last frost

Spacing: 6–12"

Growing

Statice prefers **full sun**. The soil should be of **poor or average fertility, light, sandy** and **well drained**. This plant doesn't like having its roots disturbed, so if starting it indoors, use peat pots. Germination takes 14–21 days.

Tips

Statice makes an interesting addition to any sunny border, particularly in informal gardens. It is a perennial grown as an annual.

The basal leaves of Statice form a rosette, and the flower stalks are sent up from the middle of the plant. Space the plants quite close together to make up for this lack of width.

Cut Statice for drying late in summer, before the white center has come out on the bloom. Stand the stalks in a vase with about 1" of water and they will dry quite nicely on their own as the water is used up. If it's more convenient to keep them out of the way, you can hang them upside down in a cool, dry place.

Recommended

L. sinuatum forms a basal rosette of hairy leaves. Ridged stems bear clusters of small, papery flowers in blue, purple, pink or white. 'Fortress' has strongly branching plants and flowers in several bright and pastel shades. The plants grow up to 24" tall. 'Petite Bouquet' series has compact, 12" plants with flowers in blue, purple, pink, white and yellow. 'Sunset' grows 24" tall and bears flowers in warm red, orange, peach, yellow, apricot and salmon shades.

Problems & Pests

Most problems can be avoided by providing a well-drained site and ensuring that there is good air circulation around the plants.

Stock
Matthiola

Height: 8–36" **Spread:** 12" **Flower color:** pink, purple, red, rose, white

GOOD LOOKS AND A SWEET SMELL MAKE THESE COOL-WEATHER lovers worth planting in the garden even if their time is short. They may falter when things heat up, but they're easily replaced with other annuals, such as the 'Surfinia' petunias, which will put on a show at the drop of a hat. If you lack room in your flowerbeds, start half a dozen stock plants in a large container for use in cut-flower arrangements. They will tolerate a light frost, so seed them in the garden early and enjoy.

Planting

Seeding: Indoors in mid-winter or direct sow around last-frost date. Do not cover seeds because they require light to germinate.

Planting out: After last frost

Spacing: 12"

Growing

Stock plants prefer **full sun** but tolerate partial shade. The soil should be of **average fertility,** have lots of **organic matter** worked in and be **moist** but **well drained.**

Tips

Stocks can be used in mixed beds or in mass plantings.

Night-scented Stock should be planted where its wonderful scent can be enjoyed in the evening—near windows that are left open, beside patios or along pathways. It is best to place Night-scented Stock with other plants because it tends to look wilted and bedraggled during the day but revives impressively at night.

Recommended

M. incana (Stock) has many cultivar groups with new ones introduced each year. Its colors range from pink and purple to red, rose or white. The height can be 8–36", depending on the cultivar. **'Cinderella'** series is popular. The compact plants in this series grow about 10" tall and have fragrant, colorful flowers.

M. longipetala subsp. *bicornis* (Night-scented Stock, Evening-scented Stock) has pink or purple flowers that fill the evening air with their scent. The plants grow 12–18" tall. **'Starlight Scentsation'** bears very fragrant flowers in a wide range of colors.

Problems & Pests

Root rot or other fungal problems may occur. Slugs may be attracted to young foliage.

M. incana (this page)

These plants are in the mustard family. The genus name honors Pierandrea Mattioli (1500–77), an Italian botanist.

Strawflower
Everlasting
Bracteantha (Helichrysum)

Height: 1–5' **Spread:** 12–24" **Flower color:** yellow, red, bronze, orange, pink, white, purple

STRAWFLOWER IS AN EVERLASTING THAT HAS MADE A GLORIOUS leap into the everyday garden, thanks to the art of growing by cuttings. New cultivars, such as Proven Winners' 'Golden Beauty,' boast more tidy, compact growth and make an outstanding display in containers and hanging baskets. Though deadheading is recommended to keep Strawflower plants flowering, the blooms seem to last forever, making pruning an easy job. Strawflower takes a bit of time to get going, so if you're looking for instant color, purchase plants that are already in bloom.

Planting

Seeding: Indoors in early spring; direct sow after last frost. Do not cover seeds because they require light to germinate.

Planting out: After last frost

Spacing: 10–18"

Growing

Strawflower prefers locations that receive **full sun**. The soil should be of **average fertility, neutral to alkaline, sandy, moist** and **well drained**. Strawflower is drought tolerant.

Be careful not to overwater, as overwatering will cause the leaves to turn yellow and encourages disease.

Tips

Include Strawflower in mixed beds, borders and containers. The lowest-growing varieties make useful edging plants. Taller varieties may require staking.

The most popular use of Strawflower is for fresh or dried flower arrangements.

Recommended

B. bracteata (H. bracteatum) is a tall, upright plant with gray-green foliage and brightly colored, papery flowers. The species can grow up to 5' tall, but the cultivars are generally a bit more compact. **'Bright Bikini'** series has large, colorful flowers on compact plants that grow to about 12" tall. **'Golden Beauty'** is a Proven Winners selection. It bears bright yellow flowers and is useful in containers, hanging baskets and window boxes. **'Pastel'** mixed has smaller flowers in soft tones that blend in well with other colors.

Problems & Pests

Strawflower is susceptible to downy mildew.

To dry the flowers, harvest when they are half open, before the centers are exposed. They will open fully as they dry. The stems are brittle, and if you replace them with wire, do so just after picking. If you wait until the flowers dry, they will shatter.

Sunflower

Helianthus

Height: dwarf varieties 24–36"; giants up to 15' **Spread:** 12–24"
Flower color: most commonly yellow but also orange, red, brown, cream
or bicolored; typically with brown, purple or rusty red centers

IF THE NAME SUNFLOWER CONJURES UP VISIONS OF FRIENDLY
giants with golden heads nodding in the breeze, you're a bit behind the times.
Hybridizers have had a ball with this easy-to-grow annual, and the results
have been downright stunning. The 5' 'Velvet Queen' carries elegant, dark red
flowers that will garner rave reviews when used at the back of a border.
'Valentine,' an Allan Armitage favorite, is a three to five footer that bears luscious 6" wide flowers with dark, almost black, centers. Of the short forms, my
favorite is the much-branched 'Music Box,' with its mix of yellow to
mahogany colors. These new breeds of Sunflower make great cut flowers and
many are pollenless, so they won't make messes like their granddaddies do.

Planting

Seeding: Indoors in late winter; direct sow in spring

Planting out: After last frost

Spacing: 12–24"

Growing

Sunflower grows best in **full sun**. The soil should be of **average fertility, humus rich, moist** and **well drained**.

The annual Sunflower is an excellent plant for children to grow. The seeds are big and easy to handle, and they germinate quickly. The plants grow continually upwards, and their progress can be measured until the flower finally appears on top of the tall plant. If planted along the wall of a two-story house, beneath an upstairs window, the progress can be observed from above as well as below, and the flowers will be easier to see.

H. annuus is grown as a crop for its seeds, which are used for roasting, snacking, baking or for producing oil or flour.

Tips

The lower-growing varieties can be used in beds and borders. The tall varieties are effective at the backs of borders and make good screens and temporary hedges. The tallest varieties may need staking.

Birds will flock to the ripening seedheads of your sunflowers, quickly plucking out the tightly packed seeds. If you plan to keep the seeds to eat, you may need to place a mesh net, the sort used to keep birds out of cherry trees, around the flowerheads until the seeds ripen. The net can be a bit of a nuisance and doesn't look too nice; most gardeners leave the flowers to the birds and buy seeds for eating.

Recommended

H. annuus (Common Sunflower) is considered weedy, but the development of many new cultivars has revived the use of this plant. '**Music Box**' is a branching plant that grows about 30" tall and has flowers in all colors, including some bicolors. '**Prado Red**' bears deep mahogany flowers and grows up to 5'. '**Russian Giant**' grows up to 10' tall and bears yellow flowers and large seeds. '**Teddy Bear**' has fuzzy-looking double flowers on compact plants 24–36" tall. '**Valentine**' bears creamy yellow flowers and grows up to 5'. '**Velvet Queen**' is a branching cultivar that bears many crimson red flowers.

Problems & Pests

Powdery mildew may affect these plants.

Swan River Daisy

Brachyscome (Brachycome)

Height: 8–18" **Spread:** equal to or slightly greater than height
Flower color: blue, pink, white, purple; usually with yellow centers

THIS PLANT'S DAINTY, DAISY-LIKE FLOWERS AND LACY, FERN-LIKE foliage make a winning combination. Even better, new varieties have been bred to better withstand hot summer weather, though they still enjoy protection from afternoon heat. Excellent drainage is a must, so Swan River Daisy is best used in rock gardens and as an edging plant in containers. It makes a lovely companion to gray-leaved plants, such as Dusty Miller and the perennial artemisias.

Planting

Seeding: Indoors in late winter; direct sow in mid-spring

Planting out: Early spring

Spacing: 12"

This Australian plant takes its name from the Swan, a river in southwestern Australia.

Growing

Swan River Daisy prefers **full sun** but benefits from light shade in the afternoon. The soil should be **fertile** and **well drained**. Allow the soil to dry between waterings.

Plant out early because cool spring weather encourages compact, sturdy growth. This plant is frost tolerant and tends to die back when the summer gets too hot. Cut it back if it begins to fade, and don't plant it in hot areas of the garden.

Tips

This versatile plant is useful for edging beds and works well in rock gardens, mixed containers and hanging baskets.

Combine Swan River Daisy with plants that mature later in the season. As Swan River Daisy fades in July, the companions will be filling in and beginning to flower.

The flowers are fragrant and long lasting when cut for arrangements.

Recommended

B. iberidifolia forms a bushy, spreading mound of feathery foliage. Blue-purple or pink-purple, daisy like flowers are borne all summer. **'Bravo'** bears flowers in white, blue, purple or pink and flowers profusely in a cool but bright spot in the garden. **'Splendor'** series has dark-centered flowers in pink, purple or white.

Problems & Pests

Aphids, slugs and snails cause occasional trouble for this plant.

Sweet Pea
Lathyrus

Height: 1–6' **Spread:** 6–12" **Flower color:** pink, red, purple, blue, salmon, pale yellow, peach, white or bicolored

SWEET PEA IS TO A COTTAGE GARDEN AS TOMATOES ARE TO THE vegetable patch. The secret to growing it is to get it started early. This cool-weather lover needs to do its thing before the temperatures begin reaching the 80s, when it will begin to decline. Not to worry: by that time the morning glories should be coming on. For those who haven't room to install a trellis, the non-climbing bush forms like 'Bijou' and 'Supersnoop' do nicely in containers and hanging baskets.

Planting
Seeding: Direct sow in early spring

Spacing: 6–12"

Sweet Pea blossoms make attractive, long-lasting cut flowers. Cutting the flowers encourages still more blooms.

Growing

Sweet Pea prefers **full sun** but tolerates light shade. The soil should be **fertile,** high in **organic matter, moist** and **well drained**. Fertilize very lightly with a low-nitrogen fertilizer during the flowering season. This plant will tolerate light frost. Deadhead all spent blooms.

Soak seeds in water for 24 hours or nick them with a nail file before planting them. Planting a second crop of Sweet Pea about a month after the first one will ensure a longer blooming period.

Tips

Sweet Pea will grow up poles, trellises and fences or over rocks. The low-growing varieties form low, shrubby mounds.

To help prevent diseases from afflicting your Sweet Pea plants, avoid planting in the same location two years in a row.

L. odoratus (this page), with *Stokesia* (below)

Recommended

Many cultivars of *L. odoratus* are available. '**Bijou**' series is a popular heat-resistant variety that grows 18" tall, with an equal spread. It needs no support to grow. '**Bouquet**' mixed is a tall, climbing variety. '**Supersnoop**' series is a sturdy bush type that needs no support. The flowers are fragrant. Pinch the tips of its long stems to encourage low growth.

Problems & Pests

Slugs and snails may eat the foliage of young plants. Root rot, mildew, rust and leaf spot may also afflict Sweet Pea occasionally.

Verbena
Garden Verbena
Verbena

Height: 8"–5' **Spread:** 12–36" **Flower color:** red, pink, purple, blue, yellow, scarlet, salmon, magenta, silver, peach or white; usually with white centers

UNIVERSITY OF GEORGIA HORTICULTURE PROFESSORS ALLAN Armitage and Mike Dirr were driving along the back roads of Georgia when they spied a field full of brilliant purple flowers. That trailing verbena, a chance hybrid, is now known as 'Homestead Purple' and has become the darling of the gardening world. It makes an outstanding annual groundcover and is unsurpassed as a container plant. For a knock-your-socks-off combination, pair this versatile beauty with 'Limelight' Licorice Plant. *V. bonariensis*, a tall, upright relative, makes a nice addition to the middle or back of the border in a cottage garden. It is a rather rangy plant that looks best planted in masses.

Planting

Seeding: Indoors in mid-winter

Planting out: After last frost

Spacing: 18"

Growing

Verbenas grow best in **full sun**. The soil should be **fertile** and very **well drained**. Pinch back young plants for bushy growth.

Chill seeds one week before sowing. Moisten the soil before sowing seeds. Do not cover the seeds with soil. Place the entire seed tray or pot in darkness, and water only if the soil becomes very dry. Once the seeds germinate, move them into the light.

V. x hybrida (this page)

The Romans, it is said, believed verbena could rekindle the flames of dying love. They named it Herba Veneris, *'plant of Venus.'*

V. bonariensis (this page)

Tips

Use verbenas on rock walls and in beds, borders, rock gardens, containers, hanging baskets and window boxes. They make good substitutes for Ivy-leaved Geranium where the sun is hot and where a roof overhang keeps the mildew-prone verbenas dry.

Recommended

V. bonariensis forms a low clump of foliage from which tall, stiff, flower-bearing stems emerge. The small purple flowers are held in clusters. This plant grows up to 5' tall but spreads only 18–24". This species may survive a mild winter, and it may self-seed.

V. canadensis (Clump Verbena, Rose Vervain) is a low-growing, spreading plant native to south-central and southeastern North America. It grows up to 18" tall and spreads up to 36". It bears clusters of pink flowers from mid-summer to fall and may survive a mild winter. 'Homestead Purple' is the most common cultivar; it is more common than the species in gardens. It bears dark purple flowers all summer. This cultivar is mildew resistant. Other cultivars include 'Babylon,' with light blue, lilac, magenta, pink, silver or white flowers; and 'Tukana,' with flowers in shades of blue, salmon and scarlet.

V. x hybrida is a bushy plant that may be upright or spreading. It bears clusters of small flowers in shades of white, purple, blue, pink, red or yellow. 'Peaches and Cream' is a spreading plant with flowers that open to a soft peach color and fade to white.

'**Romance**' series has red, pink, purple or white flowers, with white eyes. The plants grow to 8–10" tall. '**Showtime**' bears brightly colored flowers on compact plants that grow to 10" tall and spread 18". '**Temari**' series is mildew resistant and heat tolerant with vigorous, spreading growth. Flowers come in a range of colors.

Problems & Pests

Aphids, whiteflies, slugs and snails may be troublesome. Avoid fungal problems by making sure there is good air circulation around verbena plants.

If plants become leggy or overgrown, cut them back by one-half to tidy them up and promote lots of fall blooms.

V. x hybrida (above), *V. bonariensis* (below)

Viola
Pansy, Johnny-Jump-Up
Viola

Height: 3–10" **Spread:** 6–12" **Flower color:** blue, purple, red, orange, yellow, pink, white, multi-colored

FROM THE SWEET JOHNNY-JUMP-UP TO THE CUTE, CAT-FACED Pansy, plants in the genus *Viola* are cheery harbingers of spring. When planted in fall, newer cultivars, such as 'Icicle,' are guaranteed to overwinter and bloom again in spring. These versatile plants are perfect for planting early in the season when frost still threatens. It's a joy to see their smiling faces peeking through unexpected late-spring snowfalls, as if to reassure us warm weather is on its way.

Viola flowers are edible and make delightful garnishes on salads and desserts. Make candied violets by brushing the flowers with whipped egg white and sprinkling them with superfine sugar. Allow them to dry overnight.

Planting

Seeding: Indoors in early winter or mid-summer

Planting out: Early spring or early fall

Spacing: 6"

Growing

Violas prefer **full sun** but tolerate partial shade. The soil should be **fertile, moist** and **well drained.**

Violas do best when the weather is cool. They may die back completely in summer. Plants may rejuvenate in fall, but it is often easier to plant new ones in fall and not take up summer garden space with plants that don't look their best.

Direct sowing is not recommended. Sow seeds indoors in early winter for spring flowers and in mid-summer for fall and early-winter blooms. More seeds will germinate if they are kept in darkness until they sprout. Place seed trays in a

V. tricolor (above),
V. x *wittrockiana* at sunset (below)

dark closet or cover with dark plastic or layers of newspaper to block out the light.

Tips

Violas can be used in beds and borders, and they are popular for mixing in with spring-flowering bulbs. They can also be grown in containers. The large-flowered violas are preferred for early-spring color among primroses in garden beds.

Recommended

V. tricolor (Johnny-jump-up) is a popular species. The flowers are purple, white and yellow, usually in combination, although several varieties have flowers in a single color, often purple. This plant will thrive in gravel. **'Bowles Black'** has dark purple flowers that appear almost black. The center of each flower is yellow. **'Helen Mound'** ('Helen Mount') bears large flowers in the traditional purple, yellow and white combination.

V. x *wittrockiana* (Pansy) comes in blue, purple, red, orange, yellow, pink and white, often multi-colored or with face-like markings. **'Floral Dance'** is popular for spring and fall displays as it is quite cold hardy; it has flowers in a variety of solid colors and multi-colors. **'Imperial'**

V. x *wittrockiana* (this page), with tulips (below right)

series bears large flowers in a range of unique colors. For example, **'Imperial Frosty Rose'** has flowers with deep rose pink centers that gradually pale to white near the edges of the petals. **'Joker'** series has bicolored or multi-colored flowers with distinctive face markings. The flowers come in all colors. **'Maxim Marina'** bears light blue flowers with white-rimmed, dark blue blotches at the center. This cultivar tolerates both hot and cold temperatures. **'Watercolor'** series is a newer group of cultivars with flowers in delicate pastel shades.

V. x wittrockiana in mixed planter (above)

Problems & Pests

Slugs and snails can be problems. Fungal problems can be avoided through good air circulation and good drainage.

Collect short vases, such as perfume bottles with narrow necks, for displaying the cut flowers of violas. The more you pick, the more profusely the plants will bloom. These flowers are also among the easiest to press between sheets of wax paper, weighted down with stacks of books.

Wishbone Flower
Torenia

Height: 6–12" **Spread:** 6–12" **Flower color:** purple, pink, blue, burgundy, white, often bicolored with a yellow spot on the lower petal

WISHBONE FLOWER IS AN OLDIE BUT GOODIE THAT HYBRIDIZERS have been playing with in hopes of breeding tolerance to high heat and humidity. The 'Duchess' series is making great strides, so try this showy little annual in beds, borders and containers. Wishbone Flower is one of the few annuals that will tolerate permanently moist soil, making it ideal for low, damp spots, shaded edges of ponds and streams or even the damp soil beneath your outdoor water tap.

Planting

Seeding: Indoors in late winter

Planting out: After last frost date

Spacing: About 8"

Growing

Wishbone Flower prefers **light shade** but tolerates partial and full shade. The soil should be **fertile, light, humus rich** and **moist**. This plant requires regular watering.

Don't cover seeds when planting; they require light to germinate.

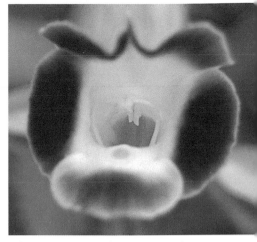

Tips

Wishbone Flower can be massed in a shaded bed or border, used as an edging plant or added to mixed containers and hanging baskets. It makes a nice change in shade gardens if you are tired of using impatiens. Try Wishbone Flower near a water feature, where the soil may remain moist for extended periods.

The stamens (male parts) in the center of the flower are arranged in the shape of a wishbone, giving rise to the common name.

Recommended

T. fournieri is a bushy, rounded to upright plant. It grows up to 12" tall, with an equal or lesser spread. Its purple flowers have yellow throats. '**Clown**' series features compact plants that grow 6–10" tall. The flowers may be purple, blue, pink or white. '**Duchess**' series has compact plants, up to 6" tall, and bears larger flowers in a range of colors.

Problems & Pests

Fungal problems can occur in overly wet soils. Moist but not soggy soils are ideal.

This plant can be potted before the frost and brought indoors to flower in a bright room.

Zinnia

Zinnia

Height: 6–36" **Spread:** 12" **Flower color:** red, yellow, green, purple, orange, pink, white, maroon, brown, gold

ONCE SO POPULAR, ZINNIAS FELL OUT OF FAVOR WHEN POWDERY mildew became troublesome back in the '60s. But when Martha Stewart featured lovely, large, lime green zinnias in a floral bouquet, American gardeners decided to give them another go. Plants of the 'Profusion' series, All-America selections in white, yellow and cherry, are the best of the best for disease tolerance, heat resistance and repeat blooming. Mexican Zinnia is great to use for border edgings and containers.

Planting

Seeding: Indoors in late winter; direct sow after last frost

Planting out: After last frost

Spacing: 6–12"

Growing

Zinnias grow best in **full sun**. The soil should be **fertile,** rich in **organic matter, moist** and **well drained.** When starting seeds indoors, plant them in individual peat pots to avoid disturbing the roots when transplanting.

Z. 'Profusion White', Z. elegans (below)

Zinnias make excellent, long-lasting cut flowers for fresh arrangements.

Deadhead zinnias to keep them flowering and looking their best. To keep mildew from the leaves, plant mildew-resistant varieties and avoid wetting the foliage when you water.

Tips

Zinnias are useful in beds, borders, containers and cutting gardens. The dwarf varieties can be used as edging plants. These plants are wonderful for fall color. Combine the rounded zinnia flowers with the spiky blooms of sun-loving salvia, or use the taller varieties in front of sunflowers.

Recommended

Z. elegans flowers come in several forms including single, double and cactus flowered. On a cactus-flowered bloom, the petals appear to be rolled into tubes like the spines of a cactus. **'California Giants'** are bushy plants growing to 36" and bearing large double flowers in a wide range of colors. **'Peter Pan'** grows up to 12" tall, but it starts blooming early at 6", with flowers in

Z. haageana cultivar (above),
Z. elegans cultivar (below)

The name Zinnia honors Johann Gottfried Zinn (1727–59), a German botany professor who first grew one of the South American zinnias from seed.

mixed colors. **'Thumbelina'** series has small flowers in all colors on dwarf, 6", weather-resistant plants.

Z. haageana (Z. angustifolia) (Mexican Zinnia) is a bushy plant with narrow leaves. It grows 6–24" tall, spreads 12" and bears bright orange, daisy-like flowers. This species is heat and drought tolerant and pest resistant. **'Crystal White'** bears white, daisy-like flowers on plants that grow 6–8" tall. It makes a wonderful edger for beds and borders. **'Persian Carpet'** bears bicolored and tricolored flowers in orange, red, yellow, maroon, brown and gold.

Z. 'Profusion' series includes fast-growing, mildew-resistant hybrids. The compact plants grow 10–18" tall and bear flowers in bright cherry red, orange or white; the individual cultivars are called '**Profusion Cherry,**' '**Profusion Orange**' and '**Profusion White.**'

Problems & Pests

Zinnias are prone to mildew and other fungal problems. Prevent such problems by ensuring good air circulation and drainage for the plants.

Z. e. 'California Giants' (above), *Z. elegans* (below)

HEIGHT LEGEND: Low: < 12" • Medium: 12–24" • Tall: > 24"

SPECIES by Common Name	COLOR									SOWING		HEIGHT		
	White	Pink	Red	Orange	Yellow	Blue	Purple	Green	Foliage	Indoors	Direct	Low	Medium	Tall
Abutilon	*	*	*	*	*					*			*	*
African Daisy	*	*	*	*	*					*	*		*	
Ageratum	*	*				*	*			*	*	*	*	*
Agrostemma	*	*					*			*	*			*
Alyssum	*	*				*	*			*	*	*		
Amaranthus		*		*				*	*	*	*			*
Angel's Trumpet	*			*	*		*			*				*
Angel Wings	*						*			*			*	
Baby's Breath	*	*					*			*	*		*	*
Bachelor's Buttons	*	*	*			*	*			*	*		*	*
Bacopa	*						*					*		
Begonia	*	*	*	*	*				*	*		*	*	
Bells-of-Ireland								*		*	*			*
Bidens					*					*	*	*		
Black-eyed Susan			*	*	*					*	*	*	*	*
Black-eyed Susan Vine	*			*	*	*	*			*	*			*
Blanket Flower			*	*	*					*	*		*	*
Blue Lace Flower	*					*				*	*		*	
Blue Marguerite	*					*	*			*	*	*	*	
Browallia	*					*	*			*		*	*	
Calendula	*			*	*					*	*	*	*	
California Poppy	*	*	*	*	*						*	*	*	
Candytuft	*	*	*				*			*	*	*		
Canterbury Bells	*	*				*	*			*			*	*
Cathedral Bells	*						*	*		*				*
China Aster	*	*	*		*	*	*			*	*	*	*	*
Chinese Forget-me-not	*	*				*				*	*		*	
Cleome	*	*					*			*	*			*
Cockscomb		*	*	*	*			*		*	*	*	*	*

Hardy	Half-hardy	Tender	Sun	Part Shade	Light Shade	Shade	Moist	Well Drained	Dry	Fertile	Average	Poor	Page Number	SPECIES by Common Name
		*	*	*			*	*		*	*		48	Abutilon
		*	*				*	*	*		*		50	African Daisy
		*	*	*			*	*		*			52	Ageratum
	*		*					*				*	56	Agrostemma
*			*		*			*			*	*	58	Alyssum
		*	*					*			*	*	60	Amaranthus
		*	*				*			*			64	Angel's Trumpet
		*	*	*			*		*	*			68	Angel Wings
*			*					*	*			*	70	Baby's Breath
*			*				*	*		*	*		72	Bachelor's Buttons
		*		*			*			*	*		74	Bacopa
		*		*	*			*		*			76	Begonia
	*		*	*			*				*		80	Bells-of-Ireland
	*		*				*	*		*			82	Bidens
	*		*	*			*	*	*		*		84	Black-eyed Susan
	*		*	*	*		*	*		*			88	Black-eyed Susan Vine
*			*					*	*		*	*	90	Blanket Flower
*			*	*				*			*		92	Blue Lace Flower
	*		*					*			*		94	Blue Marguerite
		*	*	*	*	*		*		*			96	Browallia
*			*	*				*			*		98	Calendula
*			*					*	*		*	*	100	California Poppy
*			*	*				*			*	*	102	Candytuft
*			*	*			*	*		*			104	Canterbury Bells
	*		*					*			*		108	Cathedral Bells
	*		*	*			*	*		*			110	China Aster
*			*	*			*	*			*		112	Chinese Forget-me-not
	*		*	*			*	*	*	*	*	*	114	Cleome
		*	*					*		*			118	Cockscomb

SPECIES
by Common Name

	White	Pink	Red	Orange	Yellow	Blue	Purple	Green	Foliage	Indoors	Direct	Low	Medium	Tall
Coleus							*		*	*		*	*	*
Coreopsis			*	*	*					*	*	*	*	*
Cosmos	*	*	*	*	*		*			*	*		*	*
Creeping Zinnia				*	*						*	*		
Cup Flower	*					*	*			*		*		
Dahlberg Daisy				*	*					*	*	*		
Dahlia	*	*	*	*	*		*			*	*	*	*	*
Diascia	*	*	*							*		*		
Dusty Miller	*				*				*	*			*	
Dwarf Morning Glory		*				*	*			*	*	*		
Fan Flower						*	*			*		*		
Flowering Flax	*	*	*			*	*				*		*	*
Four-o'clock Flower	*	*	*		*					*	*		*	*
Fuchsia	*	*	*	*			*			*		*	*	*
Gazania	*	*	*	*	*					*	*	*	*	
Geranium	*	*	*	*			*		*	*		*	*	*
Globe Amaranth	*	*	*				*			*		*	*	*
Godetia	*	*	*				*				*		*	*
Heliotrope	*					*	*			*		*	*	*
Hollyhock	*	*	*		*		*			*				*
Hyacinth Bean	*						*			*	*			*
Impatiens	*	*	*	*	*		*		*	*		*	*	*
Lantana	*	*	*	*	*		*			*			*	
Larkspur	*	*				*	*			*	*		*	*
Lavatera	*	*								*	*		*	*
Licorice Plant	*				*				*			*	*	
Lisianthus	*	*			*	*	*			*		*	*	
Livingstone Daisy	*	*	*	*	*					*	*	*		
Lobelia	*	*	*			*	*			*		*		

Hardy	Half-hardy	Tender	Sun	Part Shade	Light Shade	Shade	Moist	Well Drained	Dry	Fertile	Average	Poor	Page Number	SPECIES by Common Name
		*	*	*	*	*	*	*		*	*		122	Coleus
*			*						*	*	*	*	126	Coreopsis
		*	*						*	*	*		128	Cosmos
		*	*						*		*		132	Creeping Zinnia
	*		*	*			*	*			*		134	Cup Flower
*			*						*		*	*	136	Dahlberg Daisy
		*	*				*	*		*			138	Dahlia
	*		*	*			*	*		*			142	Diascia
	*		*		*				*		*		144	Dusty Miller
		*	*						*		*	*	146	Dwarf Morning Glory
		*	*		*		*				*		148	Fan Flower
*			*	*					*		*		150	Flowering Flax
		*	*	*					*		*	*	152	Four-o'clock Flower
		*		*	*		*				*		154	Fuchsia
		*	*	*	*				*	*	*		158	Gazania
		*	*	*	*			*		*			160	Geranium
		*	*					*			*		164	Globe Amaranth
*			*		*			*	*		*	*	166	Godetia
	*		*				*	*			*	*	168	Heliotrope
*			*	*				*			*	*	172	Hollyhock
	*		*				*	*			*	*	176	Hyacinth Bean
	*		*	*	*	*	*				*		178	Impatiens
	*		*	*			*	*	*	*			182	Lantana
*			*		*			*			*		184	Larkspur
*			*				*	*			*		188	Lavatera
	*		*				*	*			*	*	192	Licorice Plant
	*		*	*	*			*			*		194	Lisianthus
		*	*						*	*	*	*	196	Livingstone Daisy
*			*	*			*				*		198	Lobelia

SPECIES
by Common Name

SPECIES by Common Name	COLOR									SOWING		HEIGHT		
	White	Pink	Red	Orange	Yellow	Blue	Purple	Green	Foliage	Indoors	Direct	Low	Medium	Tall
Love-in-a-mist	*	*				*	*			*	*		*	
Marigold	*		*	*	*					*		*	*	*
Mexican Sunflower			*	*	*					*	*			*
Million Bells	*	*	*	*	*		*					*		
Monkey Flower	*	*	*	*	*		*			*		*		
Morning Glory	*	*	*	*	*	*	*		*	*	*			*
Moss Rose	*	*	*	*	*		*			*		*		
Nasturtium	*	*	*	*	*		*		*	*	*	*	*	*
Nemesia	*	*	*	*	*	*	*			*		*		
Nicotiana	*	*	*		*		*	*		*	*		*	*
Painted-tongue			*	*	*	*	*			*	*		*	
Passion Flower	*	*				*	*			*				*
Periwinkle	*	*	*				*			*		*	*	
Persian Shield							*	*			*		*	
Petunia	*	*	*		*		*			*		*	*	
Phlox	*	*	*			*	*	*			*	*	*	
Poppy	*	*	*	*	*		*				*			*
Salvia	*	*	*	*	*	*	*			*	*	*	*	*
Scabiosa	*	*				*	*	*		*	*		*	*
Snapdragon	*	*	*	*	*		*			*	*	*	*	*
Statice	*	*	*	*	*	*	*			*	*		*	
Stock	*	*	*				*			*		*	*	*
Strawflower	*	*	*	*	*		*			*	*		*	*
Sunflower			*	*	*					*	*			*
Swan River Daisy	*	*				*				*	*	*	*	
Sweet Pea	*	*	*			*	*	*			*		*	*
Verbena	*	*	*			*	*	*		*		*	*	*
Viola	*	*	*	*	*	*	*			*		*		
Wishbone Flower	*	*				*	*	*		*		*		
Zinnia	*	*	*	*	*		*	*		*	*	*	*	*

SPECIES
by Common Name

Hardy	Half-hardy	Tender	Sun	Part Shade	Light Shade	Shade	Moist	Well Drained	Dry	Fertile	Average	Poor	Page Number	Species by Common Name
*			*					*			*		200	Love-in-a-mist
	*		*					*	*		*		202	Marigold
		*	*					*	*		*	*	206	Mexican Sunflower
	*		*				*	*	*	*			208	Million Bells
	*	*		*	*		*			*			210	Monkey Flower
	*		*					*			*	*	212	Morning Glory
	*		*					*	*			*	216	Moss Rose
	*		*	*	*			*			*	*	218	Nasturtium
	*		*				*	*		*	*		222	Nemesia
	*		*	*	*		*	*		*			224	Nicotiana
	*		*					*		*			228	Painted-tongue
*				*	*		*	*			*		230	Passion Flower
	*			*	*		*	*	*	*	*	*	232	Periwinkle
	*			*	*			*		*	*		234	Persian Shield
	*		*					*		*	*		236	Petunia
*			*				*			*			240	Phlox
*			*					*		*			242	Poppy
	*	*	*		*		*			*	*		246	Salvia
	*		*				*	*		*	*		250	Scabiosa
	*		*	*	*			*		*			252	Snapdragon
	*		*					*	*		*	*	256	Statice
*				*	*		*	*			*		258	Stock
	*		*				*	*	*		*		260	Strawflower
*			*				*	*			*		262	Sunflower
	*			*	*			*		*			266	Swan River Daisy
*				*	*		*			*			268	Sweet Pea
*	*		*					*		*			270	Verbena
*				*	*		*			*			274	Viola
	*			*	*	*	*			*			278	Wishbone Flower
	*		*					*	*		*		280	Zinnia

Glossary of Terms

acid soil: soil with a pH lower than 7.0

alkaline soil: soil with a pH higher than 7.0

annual: a plant that germinates, flowers, sets seed and dies in one growing season

basal leaves: leaves that form from the crown, at the base of the plant

biennial: a plant that germinates and produces stems, roots and leaves in the first growing season; it flowers, sets seed and dies in the second growing season

crown: the part of a plant at or just below soil level where the shoots join the roots

cultivar: a cultivated plant variety with one or more distinct differences from the species, e.g., in flower color, leaf variegation or disease resistance

damping off: fungal disease causing seedlings to rot at soil level and topple over

deadhead: to remove spent flowers to maintain a ncat appearance and encourage a longer blooming period

desiccation: drying out of plant tissue, especially foliage

direct sow: to sow seeds directly in the garden soil where the plants are to grow, as opposed to sowing first in pots or flats and transplanting

disbud: to remove some flower buds to improve the size or quality of the remaining ones

dormancy: a period of plant inactivity, usually during winter or unfavorable climatic conditions

double flower: a flower with an unusually large number of petals, often caused by mutation of the stamens into petals

forma (f.): a naturally occurring variant of a species; below the level of subspecies in biological classification and similar to variety

genus: a category of biological classification between the species and family levels; the first word in a scientific name indicates the genus

half-hardy: a plant capable of surviving the climatic conditions of a given region if protected from heavy frost or cold

harden off: to gradually acclimatize plants that have been growing in a protective environment (usually indoors) to a more harsh environment (usually outdoors in spring)

hardy: capable of surviving unfavorable conditions, such as cold weather or frost, without protection

humus: decomposed or decomposing organic material in the soil

hybrid: a plant resulting from natural or human-induced cross-breeding between varieties, species or genera; the hybrid expresses features of each parent plant

neutral soil: soil with a pH of 7.0

node: the area on a stem from which a leaf or new shoot grows

pH: a measure of acidity or alkalinity (the lower the pH, the higher the acidity); the pH of soil influences availability of nutrients for plants

perennial: a plant that takes three or more years to complete its life cycle; a herbaceous perennial normally dies back to the ground over winter

potager: a garden that combines function with beauty, often by growing vegetables, herbs and ornamental flowers together in a formal pattern of raised beds

quilled: the narrow, tubular shape of petals or florets of certain flowers

rhizome: a root-like food-storing stem that grows horizontally at or just below soil level, from which new shoots may emerge

rootball: the root mass and surrounding soil of a plant

runner: a modified stem that grows on the soil surface; roots and new shoots are produced at nodes along its length

semi-double flower: a flower with petals that form two or three rings

sepal: segment of the outermost ring of a typical flower; usually green and leaf-like, but may be large, colorful and petal-like

single flower: a flower with a single ring of typically four or five petals

species: the fundamental unit of biological classification, simply defined as a group of interfertile organisms; the original entity from which cultivars and varieties are derived

subshrub: a plant that is somewhat shrubby or woody at the base; tender subshrubs may be grown as annuals

subspecies (subsp.): a naturally occurring, regional form of a species, often isolated from other subspecies but still potentially interfertile with them

taproot: a root system consisting of one long main root with smaller roots branching from it

tender: incapable of surviving the climatic conditions of a given region and requiring protection from frost or cold

tepal: a sepal or petal of a flower, when the petals and sepals are not clearly distinguished from each other

true: the passing of desirable characteristics from the parent plant to seed-grown offspring; also called breeding true to type

tuber: the thick section of a rhizome bearing nodes and buds

variegation: foliage that has more than one color, often patched or striped or bearing differently colored leaf margins

variety (var.): a naturally occurring variant of a species; below the level of subspecies in biological classification

xeriscape: a landscaping method that conserves water by using native and drought-tolerant plants

The following mail-order companies provide a wide variety of flower, vegetable and herb seeds and gardening supplies. Most will provide a catalog free of charge.

Burpee Seeds
800-888-1447
www.burpee.com

Johnny's Selected Seeds
207-437-4301
www.johnnyseeds.com

Peaceful Valley Farm Supply
888-784-1722
www.groworganic.com

Richters Herbs
905-640-6677
www.richters.com

Seeds of Change
888-762-7333
www.seedsofchange.com

Territorial Seed Co.
541-942-9547
www.territorial-seed.com

Veseys Seeds
800-363-7333
www.veseys.com

Index

Page numbers in **boldface** indicate main flower headings.